Square Pegs

Building Success in School and Life through MI

Jean Bowen
Marianne Hawkins
Carol King

Zephyr
Press ®

REACHING THEIR HIGHEST POTENTIAL

Square Pegs
Building Success in School and life through MI

Grades 4–12

Easily adaptable for grades K through 3

©1997 by Zephyr Press
Printed in the United States of America

ISBN 1-56976-075-6

Editors: Veronica Durie and Stacey Shropshire
Cover design: Dan Miedaner
Design and production: Daniel Miedaner
Illustrations: Jean Bowen
Typesetting: Daniel Miedaner

Zephyr Press
P.O. Box 66006
Tucson, AZ 85728-6006
http://www.zephyrpress.com

Library of Congress Cataloging-in-Publication Data

Bowen, Jean, 1935-
    Square pegs : building success in school and life through MI /
Jean Bowen, Marianne Hawkins, Carol King.
        p.   cm.
    Includes bibliographical references.
    ISBN 1-56976-075-6
    1. Cognitive styles. 2. Learning, Psychology of. 3. Activity
programs in education. I. Hawkins, Marianne, 1944- . II. King,
Carol, 1952- . III. Title.
BF311.B644 1997
370.15'23—DC21   97-24342

Contents

Acknowledgments

We first thank the students, families, faculty, and staff of The Howard School. Without their joy in the process of learning this work could not exist. We also thank our director, Sandra Kleinman, who offered continual encouragement. A special mention goes to Peter Dyer and Kathleen Goble, each of whom lent their technical knowledge and extraordinary patience to getting the final manuscript to press. We thank Henry and Helen Maddox, who introduced us to the art of the mandala. Through them we met Donna Pickens, who generously shared her talent as an artist to guide our students in developing their first mandalas.

We recognize the extraordinary minds of those who have inspired and molded our thinking over the years, many of whom are mentioned in our list of references. In particular, we want to pay homage to the following people: Howard Gardner, Martin Seligman, and Lynda Miller. Gardner has provided educators with a framework for a new way of thinking about intelligence. This thinking has created a fertile environment for all people to accept and value differences. Seligman's many years of looking at the need for human beings to take control of their own destiny gave us the courage throughout our professional careers to diverge from the purely academic. Miller came to us at a time when we were ready to go beyond ideas and move into action. Her materials and strategies for applying this new thinking opened a floodgate of creativity for us.

We hope that those who use this book will find it a resource to continue the chain of questions and ideas that lead to lifelong successful learning for all children.

Preface

> **Carol:** *But Sue, what is it that makes school so difficult for you?*
>
> **Sue:** *I have a real problem learning things. I have to go over and over them. I need more help than most students and math is so hard. I just don't feel like other people. I feel different and that feels bad. I don't know how to make it better.*

It is August and Carol King is meeting each of her new students individually for the first time. Listening to Sue confirms for Carol once again that we have made the right decision for the coming school year.

Carol is the teacher, the person who will take primary responsibility for the students who will be in her class. Marianne Hawkins, a language and speech specialist, will provide specific language remediation and contribute her expertise to our planning sessions. I, their former principal, will be offering supplementary instruction and an objective eye for collecting and documenting the program as it unfolds.

This new way of seeing and teaching students has evolved for us over the last ten years and is based upon the theory of multiple intelligences. We have worked as a team, experimenting with various approaches and activities, documenting those that have been successful and discarding others. We have adapted and made changes to meet each student's needs. One adaptation we have made has been to separate mathematical and logical functions. Although the same brain processes are used in both functions, we use *mathematical* to apply to anything having to do with numbers, and *logical* to refer to problem solving, sequencing, and other such thought processes. Armed with this theoretical base, Carol now feels confident and ready to change her basic teaching style. She will become the facilitator in a wonderful voyage of discovery for the three of us, her students, and their parents.

The anxiety that we feel about embarking upon this adventure is outweighed by exhilaration and the anticipation of discovery. As part of preparation we have explored our own unique learning styles and found that our approach (not only to teaching, but to many areas of life) has been dramatically altered. We believe that every human being is unique and special, and that it is the teacher's responsibility to help develop that individual potential in every child. We are now eager to share our experiences with our colleagues as a way of saying "Thank you" for providing so much of the creativity and caring we have drawn upon in reaching our personal conclusions.

Introduction

*We must stop asking how smart people are
and start asking how people are smart.*

—Howard Gardner, Harvard Project Zero

Howard Gardner's vanguard book *Frames of Mind* (1983) was a revelation to educators in general, and it was particularly meaningful to those of us who teach students with diagnosed learning differences. Armed with this new way of seeing, we strode forth with confidence and mission. The discovery that this adventure demanded far more than mission was sobering and thought provoking. Gradually, it became clear that success depended upon a willingness to look at students through a new, wider lens (see figure 1). This new way of seeing required us to take a major leap of faith.

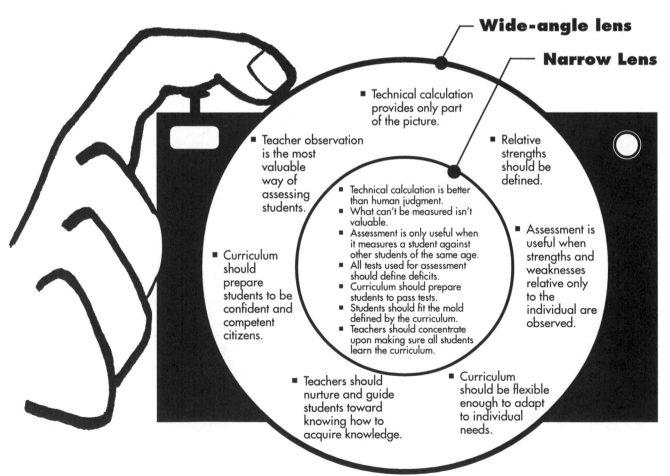

Wide-angle lens

Narrow Lens

- Technical calculation provides only part of the picture.

- Teacher observation is the most valuable way of assessing students.

- Relative strengths should be defined.

- Technical calculation is better than human judgment.
- What can't be measured isn't valuable.
- Assessment is only useful when it measures a student against other students of the same age.
- All tests used for assessment should define deficits.
- Curriculum should prepare students to pass tests.
- Students should fit the mold defined by the curriculum.
- Teachers should concentrate upon making sure all students learn the curriculum.

- Assessment is useful when strengths and weaknesses relative only to the individual are observed.

- Curriculum should prepare students to be confident and competent citizens.

- Teachers should nurture and guide students toward knowing how to acquire knowledge.

- Curriculum should be flexible enough to adapt to individual needs.

Figure 1. The wide lens, narrow lens comparison

The most significant discovery was understanding that our training and experience had required us to measure our students against other students of the same age. As we became willing to look through the wide-angle multiple intelligence lens, we saw each student's strengths relative only to that individual. For us, relinquishing old ideas and embracing new ones was essential for success in applying this new way of looking at children. Ironically, this relinquishment may have been the most difficult part of the new philosophy.

In reading Howard Gardner, we discovered that each of us has a unique combination of intelligences that vary according to situations and that will change over a lifetime. In approaching the concept of intelligence in this way we need to accept the importance of looking at the whole individual.

To the traditional areas of linguistic and logical-mathematical intelligence, Gardner adds those outlined in figure 2.

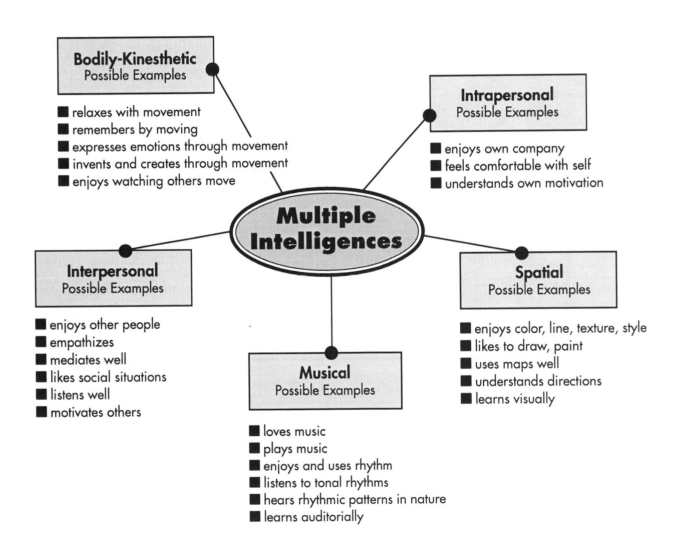

Bodily-Kinesthetic
Possible Examples
- relaxes with movement
- remembers by moving
- expresses emotions through movement
- invents and creates through movement
- enjoys watching others move

Intrapersonal
Possible Examples
- enjoys own company
- feels comfortable with self
- understands own motivation

Multiple Intelligences

Interpersonal
Possible Examples
- enjoys other people
- empathizes
- mediates well
- likes social situations
- listens well
- motivates others

Musical
Possible Examples
- loves music
- plays music
- enjoys and uses rhythm
- listens to tonal rhythms
- hears rhythmic patterns in nature
- learns auditorially

Spatial
Possible Examples
- enjoys color, line, texture, style
- likes to draw, paint
- uses maps well
- understands directions
- learns visually

Figure 2. Web of multiple intelligences

This broader look expands the camera lens and places equal value on each intelligence. We may see that an individual who does not excel linguistically or logically-mathematically may have ability in the bodily-kinesthetic or spatial intelligence. Another may be a talented people watcher or have unusual insights into personal feelings or the feelings of others, or may find a special enjoyment in contributing to the community. Yet another may have a special ability to communicate in mime or drama or may make surprising intellectual connections in lateral rather than sequential ways. When all these areas have equal worth, students not only *feel* valued but *are* valued by their peers. Their strengths are recognized and prized in a new light.

We believe that teaching students how they may identify the different ways they, and others, are smart leads to the ability to set realistic goals and to be resilient in the face of failure. Such students feel a strong internal locus of control and are able to set and reach goals (see figure 3).

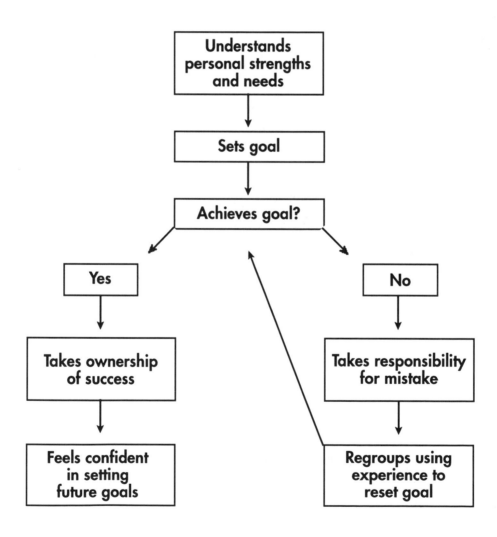

Figure 3. Resilient goal setting

Some of society's most intuitive people watchers are our most gifted cartoonists. If we look closely at the work of Charles Schultz, for example, we repeatedly see both externally and internally controlled personalities depicted in the form of Charlie Brown and Linus. Charlie seems to be in a perpetual state of astonishment at the things that happen to him, while Linus takes charge, exuding optimism and confidence about his decisions. Charlie laments to Linus that he doesn't know what to do when he feels that no one likes him. He asks Linus for advice, and Linus responds with characteristic confidence, saying that he would look at himself objectively and see what he must do to improve the situation.

As the adults who are involved in the lives of young people we believe we should help them develop the Linus characteristics, those of the successful student (see figure 4). It is upon this belief that our approach to teaching is founded and that this text is written.

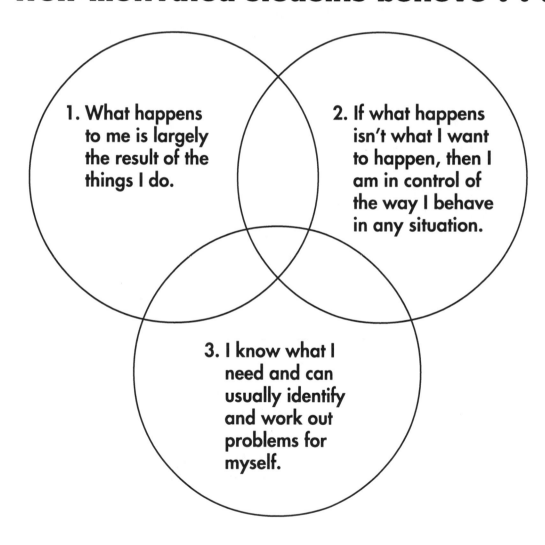

Well-motivated students believe . . .

1. What happens to me is largely the result of the things I do.

2. If what happens isn't what I want to happen, then I am in control of the way I behave in any situation.

3. I know what I need and can usually identify and work out problems for myself.

Figure 4. The well-motivated student

In implementing a program that would incorporate this new thinking we realized that we needed to make major changes in the classroom schedule. Our goals became the following:

- to allocate specific, regular times to introduce each concept
- to develop activities that integrated concepts and vocabulary into academic subjects
- to establish a classroom culture that accepts and celebrates differences
- to model our own willingness to be flexible, rebounding from failure to try again and learn something new
- to give students the knowledge they need to nurture a feeling of empowerment that, in turn, leads to motivation

How to Use This Book

This text consists of a series of teaching units designed to be integrated into an existing academic curriculum. The concepts are meant to be taught in the classroom and are cumulative; each new concept builds upon those it follows. As concepts are introduced, the ideas, behaviors, vocabulary and language are designed to be incorporated into daily activities.

Each unit consists of the following elements:

Rationale
The topic and purpose of the unit and its evolution

Teaching the Activity
Specific directions for teaching each activity

Guided Questionings
Suggested dialogue, based on transcripts from classroom dialogues, for introducing each new concept; presented as bulleted lists to indicate pauses for student responses or shifts in direction

Student Activity Sheets
Reproducible work sheets

Wall posters and teacher resource sheets are also included with some of the activities. The wall posters are visual cues to enlarge and post, if you wish. Teacher resource sheets offer information relevant to specific activities.

We suggest that you read through the guided questions before teaching the activity to become familiar with the concepts being presented. These questions are transcripts made from video tapes of actual lessons. They are meant to be used as a guide of how to present the concept and not as a script to be read during the activity. You, your students, and your situation will require you to adapt our suggestions to meet your needs.

Why Use Guided Questioning When Teaching Concepts?
Our personal experience tells us that using a questioning technique that leads students to discover concepts for themselves results in deeper, more permanent learning. This technique is based upon Bloom's taxonomy of educational objectives (see figure 5).

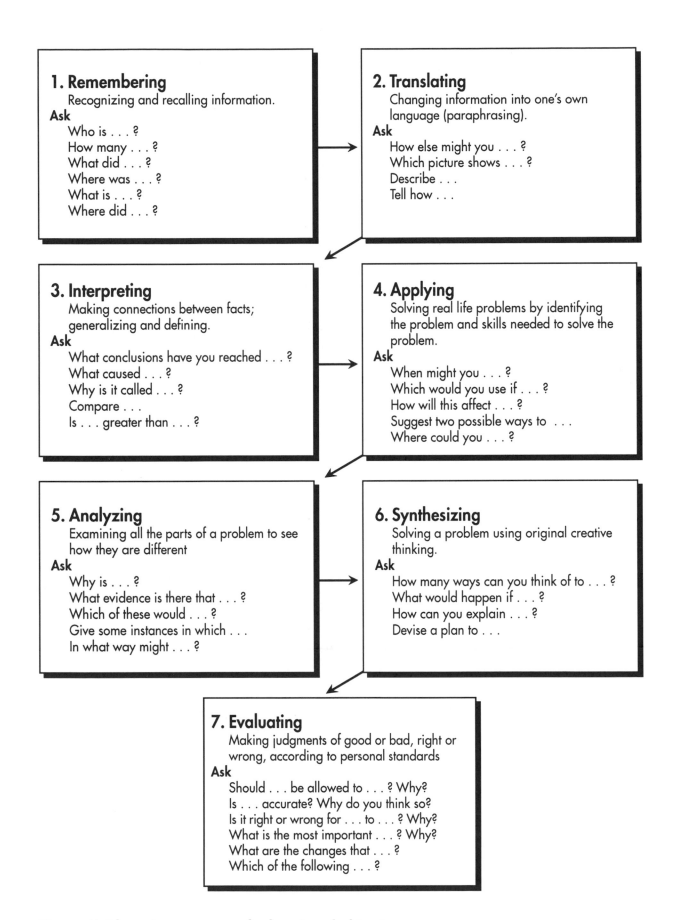

1. Remembering
Recognizing and recalling information.
Ask
    Who is . . . ?
    How many . . . ?
    What did . . . ?
    Where was . . . ?
    What is . . . ?
    Where did . . . ?

2. Translating
Changing information into one's own language (paraphrasing).
Ask
    How else might you . . . ?
    Which picture shows . . . ?
    Describe . . .
    Tell how . . .

3. Interpreting
Making connections between facts; generalizing and defining.
Ask
    What conclusions have you reached . . . ?
    What caused . . . ?
    Why is it called . . . ?
    Compare . . .
    Is . . . greater than . . . ?

4. Applying
Solving real life problems by identifying the problem and skills needed to solve the problem.
Ask
    When might you . . . ?
    Which would you use if . . . ?
    How will this affect . . . ?
    Suggest two possible ways to . . .
    Where could you . . . ?

5. Analyzing
Examining all the parts of a problem to see how they are different
Ask
    Why is . . . ?
    What evidence is there that . . . ?
    Which of these would . . . ?
    Give some instances in which . . .
    In what way might . . . ?

6. Synthesizing
Solving a problem using original creative thinking.
Ask
    How many ways can you think of to . . . ?
    What would happen if . . . ?
    How can you explain . . . ?
    Devise a plan to . . .

7. Evaluating
Making judgments of good or bad, right or wrong, according to personal standards
Ask
    Should . . . be allowed to . . . ? Why?
    Is . . . accurate? Why do you think so?
    Is it right or wrong for . . . to . . . ? Why?
    What is the most important . . . ? Why?
    What are the changes that . . . ?
    Which of the following . . . ?

Figure 5. Bloom's taxonomy of educational objectives

UNIT 1

Introducing the Concept of Multiple Intelligences

Rationale

Our experience is that students who have not been successful in school often assume that failure is the result of low intelligence. We believe that teaching about how we are different and examining the ways in which we can be smart defuses anxiety and opens the door to learning.

By taking students into the loop of knowledge, we demonstrate our respect for their ability to understand. Reinforcing the concept that intelligence is a constantly fluid process that changes throughout life nurtures students' self-esteem. Accepting that we use and adapt our intelligences to the various situations in which we find ourselves encourages the concept of an internal locus of control. Understanding that each individual is unique and has something to contribute invites the development of complementary team building and the acceptance of the notion that difference is valuable.

For us, the concept of multiple intelligences has become the foundation on which a bank of information leading to self-understanding can be built. Armed with new information and confidence, students for whom repeated failure has developed a cycle of learned helplessness can be gently nudged toward making personal choices based on knowledge.

Student Comment

What do I do if I see an intelligence in more than one place? I see my spatial intelligence in my head and in my arm, but when I use my arm it's bodily. Wait a minute! Maybe it's all in more than one place. Maybe all the intelligences are everywhere all the time. I can use them just when I want to use them.

••• Activity 1 •••

Introducing Multiple Intelligences

Student Objective
- To understand the concept of multiple intelligences

Materials
guided questioning 1, Introducing Multiple Intelligences
teacher resource sheet 1, Using Music in the Classroom
student activity sheet 1, Ways We Are Smart Interview
student activity sheets 2-1 through 2-8 (packet), Thinking about Intelligences
whiteboard or blackboard
poster board
colored markers
scissors
magazines for cutting out pictures
a chapter book

Teaching the Activity
Introduce the concept of multiple intelligences using guided questioning 2, Introducing Multiple Intelligences. Have students work in teams to develop webs of famous people who represent all the intelligences. Tell students that they may use words, or draw or cut out pictures or graphics for their maps; the only rule is that each map look attractive when it is finished.

Ask each team to choose a representative to present the web to the class when it is finished. After students have completed their webs, bring the class together and ask each group representative to present the group's map. Allow time for questions and comments from the class.

Have students work in pairs to interview each other and fill out student activity sheet 1, Ways We Are Smart Interview. Give students the packet of student activity sheet 2, Thinking about Intelligences, and have them work in pairs or individually to complete the packet. This is also an excellent time to introduce *All Kinds of Minds* or any chapter book that presents an assortment of various characters. Read the book aloud to the class every day and discuss all the characters from a multiple intelligences point of view.

A Word about the Smart Profile

The smart profile is a visual representation of an individual's relative strengths and is a tool for discovery and discussion. To this point in history educators and students have developed in a "culture of measurement." We strive to be part of the movement to change this view of the educational establishment.

Our experience is that students, parents, and teachers continue to ask questions such as, "Where am I now?" "Where do I need to be?" and, "How can I get where I need to be?" We believe that it is important for us to defuse anxiety by providing honest answers to these questions that point the way for a change in thinking. The Smart Profile is an alternative way to answer these questions by providing a picture that says, "You are here now." What we must add is that this representation is a snapshot of only this moment in time, and in this situation. We must never stop reinforcing the wide-angle concepts of change, flexibility, and individual, personal choice.

Guided Questioning 1, Introducing Multiple Intelligences

Create pictures, diagrams, and webs as the discussion evolves.

- Has anyone here ever wondered about how we measure intelligence?

Accept all ideas and encourage questions.

- Well, there is a very interesting story attached to it, and I want to share what I know about it with you. Don't worry about remembering names or anything like that. I am just going to try to give you the big idea. Okay?

Write WISC on the board.

- The test that is used most often to measure intelligence is called the Weschier Intelligence Scale for Children, or WISC for short. This test is based on looking at how well we understand words and how language works, and how well we can use numbers and logical thinking.
- Give me some examples of how we use words and language in our lives.
- Good ways. There are any different ways we use and need language. How about logic? Does anyone know what *logic* means?

Encourage as much discussion as possible that leads to understanding that logic deals with order, number, cause and effect, and sequence.

- All your ideas are good. Logic means careful, sensible thinking. How we think about things and solve problems.
- Someone give me a problem. Any problem. Something you had to do last week that took some thought.

You may have to provide a personal problem first as a model for how you reached a solution through logical thinking.

- Good one. How did you solve the problem?
- You used logic to solve your problem. Great! We use logic all the time. So it's definitely important.
- Let's agree that language and logic are both important. But how do you think people are intelligent in other ways?
- Good ideas. Some people have been looking at the different ways we are intelligent. The person that we are most interested in is a man named Howard Gardner. Dr. Gardner believes that all human beings are intelligent in multiple, or many, ways. His theory of intelligence is called *multiple intelligence theory*.
- Okay, let's try this. I'm going to name different kinds of jobs people do. See if you can come up with the kind of intelligence or intelligences that people need to use to do each job. Here we go. What kind of intelligence do you think someone would have to have to be the leader of a musical group?
- Gardner believes that being intelligent *musically* is just as important as being intelligent *linguistically* and *logically* or *mathematically*.

Write these four intelligences on the board. You may decide that this is a good time to start building a web diagram of the intelligences (see figure 6). Continue to work through the other intelligences in the same way, adding each to the web as you proceed. Whenever possible, lead students to identify the actual name of each intelligence by providing examples such as athlete, dancer—bodily; architect, decorator, artist, explorer—spatial; TV interviewer—interpersonal; research scientist—intrapersonal.

- You have named many different ways that human beings are intelligent. Gardner believes that there may be many more. Let's try and come up with a job for someone that likes to use linguistic intelligence. Any ideas?

Wait for response. Possible choices are writer, poet, editor. When an appropriate opportunity presents itself, ask students if a particular job requires more than one intelligence.

- Does being a successful athlete require only bodily-kinesthetic intelligence?

It may be appropriate to call on an athlete in the class to suggest and explain other intelligences that are required in some specific athletics. Suggestions include the following:

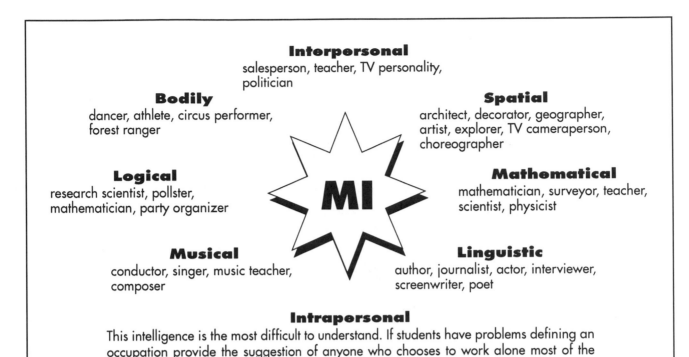

Interpersonal
salesperson, teacher, TV personality,
politician

Bodily
dancer, athlete, circus performer,
forest ranger

Spatial
architect, decorator, geographer,
artist, explorer, TV cameraperson,
choreographer

Logical
research scientist, pollster,
mathematician, party organizer

MI

Mathematical
mathematician, surveyor, teacher,
scientist, physicist

Musical
conductor, singer, music teacher,
composer

Linguistic
author, journalist, actor, interviewer,
screenwriter, poet

Intrapersonal
This intelligence is the most difficult to understand. If students have problems defining an
occupation provide the suggestion of anyone who chooses to work alone most of the
time, or who requires a lot of reflection time to do a job. Explain that this intelligence is a
thoughtful one. We use intrapersonal intelligence when we think and plan carefully. In time
students will realize that intrapersonal intelligence figures highly in most things we do.

Figure 6. The multiple intelligences and careers

- **Linguistic and interpersonal to communicate needs.**
- **Intrapersonal to think about and plan moves.**
- **Logical to plan the sequence of moves.**

Help students understand that each of us possesses all of the intelligences to some degree. In that way we are all the same, but we each have different preferences about which intelligences we like to use and different skill levels, and that is how we are different.

- Throughout the year we will be talking a lot about the different ways people are smart. We will be doing a lot of work to learn how each of us uses our various intelligences and then developing some ways of using those intelligences to be good learners.
- Let's suppose for a minute. What do you think I would do if I were very strong musically and I were asked to write a report. How do you think I could use my musical intelligence when I do my report? At first there doesn't seem to be much of a connection between musical and linguistic intelligence. Could I make one in some way?

- Good idea. I could bring them together and write a rap for my report. What intelligence do you think I would use to help me get organized?
- Good, definitely my logical intelligence. How about the way I would arrange the information on the page?
- Yes, out would come my spatial intelligence.
- So we always have to adapt. We are never able to use only one intelligence, even if it's a very strong one for us. We are still using most of the others to some degree all the time. We can't always use only what we consider our strongest intelligence.

Continue the discussion as long as time allows. Encourage students to share their ideas. Work at drawing out those students who are not linguistic. Have all students create a visual symbol or picture to represent each intelligence.

Using Music in the Classroom

Choosing Music

Music can be helpful in setting the mood for classroom work. Different music evokes different moods. Consider what mood you want to evoke before choosing music.

Baroque Music is balanced and somewhat systematic. It tends to create calm and a restful alertness. It is ideal background music.

- ◆ Examples: pieces by Bach, Correlli, Couperin, Handel, Purcell, Telemann, Vivaldi

Classical Music is full of energy, surprises, and contrasts. It's good as background music for creativity, storytelling, and lectures.

- ◆ Examples: pieces by Mozart, Hayden, Rossini, Beethoven

    Note: Recent research shows that listening to Mozart can change brain waves and help students produce positive results on tests.

Romantic Music suggests passion, suspense, wonder, and freedom. You can use it to set the background for drama and fantasy. This music clears the head of anger and frustration and evokes interest and curiosity.

- ◆ Examples: pieces by Berlioz, Brahms, Chopin, Debussy, Dvoarak, Liszt, Mendelssohn, Rimsky-Korsakov, Schubert, Schumann, Tchaikovsky, Wagner, Verdi

Post-Romantic and Early American Music includes marches, ragtime, and waltzes. Much of this music is grandiose, emotional, humorous, and exciting. Many students will recognize familiar folk songs within the music.

- ◆ Examples: pieces by Barber, Copland, Gershwin, Ives, S. Joplin, MacDowell, M. Ravel, Sousa, Strauss

Modern, Popular Music can be used at the beginning of the day to give students positive or inspirational messages to set the mood for the day. It can be used at transition times to help calm, change moods, or inspire optimism. At the end of the day, it can serve as a celebration of success or to set a positive tone.

Ways to Use Music in the Classroom:

Signal an activity change	Provide background
Calm students	Brainstorm
Celebrate successes	Begin or end the day
Inspire	Focus attention

Ways We Are Smart Interview

Name _____ Date _____

Name of interviewer _____

1. What new thing would you love to be able to do or learn?
   _____

2. What do you choose when you can do anything you like?
   _____

3. What do you not like to do?
   _____

4. When do you feel the most happy and relaxed?
   _____

5. What would you say or do if you got lost on a field trip?
   _____

6. What would it be like if your teacher were absent for a whole month?

   _____
   _____
   _____
   _____
   _____
   _____
   _____
   _____
   _____

     Square Pegs, ©1997 Zephyr Press, Tucson, Arizona

Spatial Intelligence

Name _____ Date _____

1. At this moment the inside of my desk looks

   _____

   _____

   _____

2. My desk looks this way because

   _____

   _____

   _____

3. I notice what people are wearing because

   _____

   _____

   _____

4. When I go to a new place the things I remember about it later are

   _____

   _____

   _____

5. When I am asked to build something I feel

   _____

   _____

   _____

   _____

6. I like to rearrange the furniture and items in my bedroom because it makes me feel

_____

_____

   I never rearrange my bedroom furniture because

_____

_____

7. In art I love

_____

_____

_____

8. This is the way I feel about these things

Movies	not interested	interested	very interested
Video games	not interested	interested	very interested
Cartoons	not interested	interested	very interested
Graphics	not interested	interested	very interested

9. My favorite spatial activity is

_____

_____

_____

10. My spatial intelligence goal is

_____

_____

_____

_____

_____

Square Pegs, ©1997 Zephyr Press, Tucson, Arizona

Bodily-Kinesthetic Intelligence

Name _____ Date _____

1. I enjoy doing or watching the following activities:

   Sports or games because

   _____

   _____

   Movement or dance because

   _____

   _____

   Acting things out or puppet shows because

   _____

   _____

2. The following statements are true or false about me

   ■ I need to be moving in order to think well.   **T**   **F**

   ■ I feel relaxed after I move.   **T**   **F**

   ■ I remember best when I touch and move.   **T**   **F**

3. My bodily-kinesthetic intelligence goal is

   _____

   _____

   _____

   _____

Mathematical Intelligence

Name _____ Date _____

1. The way I feel about working on the mathematical skill of *estimating* is

   _____

   _____

   because _____

   _____

2. Guess the following, then circle whether it was easy or difficult for you to guess accurately.

   ■ The number of erasers that measure the length of the board: _____

                         Easy   Difficult

   ■ The number of rods in the jar: _____

                         Easy   Difficult

3. The items that I feel would cost less than $25.00 are

   candy   book

   baseball game   ball

   Battleship   pencil

4. The tasks that I believe could be accomplished in less than 15 minutes are

   running a mile

   reading a comic

   eating dinner

   taking a shower

   reading a book of 100 pages

Square Pegs, ©1997 Zephyr Press, Tucson, Arizona

5. My mathematical intelligence goal is

_____

_____

_____

_____

Use this space to demonstrate your mathematical intelligence in any way you like.

Interpersonal Intelligence

Name _____ Date _____

1. When I interviewed my classmate, I noticed that _____
   _____

2. When I interviewed my classmate, I felt _____
   _____

3. When I notice that a person has a problem, I want to _____
   _____

4. My opinion of studying people in other lands is _____
   _____

5. When I cannot be with my friends I _____
   _____

6. I think teasing is _____
   _____

7. I think problem solving with a group is useful because _____
   _____

8. My perfect day would be _____
   _____

9. My interpersonal intelligence goal is _____
   _____
   _____
   _____
   _____

   Square Pegs, ©1997 Zephyr Press, Tucson, Arizona

Linguistic Intelligence

Name _____ Date _____

1. I think reading is _____

   because _____

2. I think writing is _____

   because _____

3. I think spelling is _____

   because _____

4. When I am asked to speak in front of a group I feel _____

   because _____

5. I think the lyrics of songs are_____

   because _____

6. I think TV programs and movies with a lot of talking are _____

   because _____

7. When I hear poetry and rhyming I feel _____

   because _____

8. When I listen to stories I feel _____

   because _____

9. When I hear jokes that use language I think_____

   because _____

10. My linguistic intelligence goal is

_____

_____

_____

_____

_____

Use these lines to write something. It can be a story, poem, or anything that uses the linguistic intelligence.

_____

_____

_____

_____

_____

_____

_____

_____

_____

_____

_____

_____

_____

_____

_____

_____

_____

Square Pegs, ©1997 Zephyr Press, Tucson, Arizona

Logical Intelligence

Name _____ Date _____

1. My feelings about science are _____
   _____
   because _____

2. My feelings about computers are _____
   _____
   because _____

3. When I need to develop a plan or system to get something done I feel _____
   _____
   because _____

4. Putting things in order makes me feel _____
   _____
   because _____

5. Having a tidy desk makes me feel _____
   _____
   because _____

6. Describe or use extra paper to draw a picture of the way your room is organized.
   _____

7. My logical intelligence goal is _____
   _____
   _____
   _____

Intrapersonal Intelligence

Name _____ Date _____

1. When I first came to a new school I felt _____
   _____

   because _____

2. The idea of solving a problem alone makes me feel _____
   _____

   because _____

3. Working on projects by myself makes me feel _____
   _____

   because _____

4. When I don't know how to do something I feel _____
   _____

   because _____

5. When people ask me what I want I feel _____
   _____

   because _____

6. When people ask me what I need I feel_____
   _____

   because _____

7. My intrapersonal intelligence goal is _____
   _____
   _____
   _____

  Square Pegs, ©1997 Zephyr Press, Tucson, Arizona

Musical Intelligence

Name _____ Date _____

1. When I am concentrating, music makes me feel _____
   _____
   _____

2. I often have tunes going around in my head, or I hum as I work.

                   Yes   **No**

3. I am aware of music in the environment.

                   Yes   **No**

4. If I memorize by putting vocabulary words or spelling to music I feel _____
   _____
   _____

   because _____
   _____

5. I can make music by singing or playing an instrument.

                   Yes   **No**

6. Music can change my mood

                   Yes   **No**

7. My musical intelligence goal is _____
   _____
   _____
   _____
   _____

⚫⚫⚫ **Activity 2** ⚫⚫⚫

Profiling a Situation

Student Objectives

- To understand the concept that different situations require us to use different combinations of intelligences
- To begin to develop the ability to recognize what combinations of intelligences are required in different situations

Materials

guided questioning 2, Adapting Combinations of Intelligences
student activity sheet 3, Situations to Profile
student activity sheet 4, Profiling a Situation
3-by-5-inch index cards

Teaching the Activity

Introduce the concept using guided questioning 2, Adapting Combinations of Intelligences. Have students work separately or in pairs to prepare a stack of index cards on each of which they will write a specific situation from student activity sheet 3, Situations to Profile. Encourage them to add their own suggestions of situations. Based on the chemistry of the group, you may choose to make this into a competitive game by awarding points for original ideas.

Once students have completed these packs, you may use the packs for various games. For example, teams or individuals may take turns drawing cards, then acting out or demonstrating the combination of intelligences they used. The other team or the group guesses the situation. Or they may take turns drawing cards, then fill in student activity sheet 4, Profiling a Situation, for each situation. The latter game is especially useful to provide practice so students fully understand the concept.

Guided Questioning 2, Adapting Combinations of Intelligences

- I think you have all caught on really quickly to this whole idea of multiple intelligences. So I want us to continue with a new thought about it all. We have decided that we all use all of the different intelligences to some degree most of the time. Now, here's a challenge. See what you think about it. Einstein is sitting all alone in his study trying to work out a mathematical formula to prove one of his ideas. What intelligences is he using?
- Right, definitely mathematical. Anything else?
- Logical. Good. Anything else?
- I like that. He has the radio on so he's using musical. Anything else?
- Good, intrapersonal. That's the one I was thinking of. Why do you think he's using intrapersonal?
- Yes, he is doing a lot of problem solving and thinking and those are both very intrapersonal. Now another situation for Albert. He is arguing with another mathematician. He is trying desperately to convince this person that his new formula is correct and important. Which intelligences is he using now?
- Very good, and fast. Interpersonal. Why?

- I agree, he must be using his interpersonal and linguistic intelligences to communicate with this other person. Do you think he is using his intrapersonal intelligence as much as when he was working on his formula?

- Probably not. How about logical intelligence?

- Yes, he does have to use logical to make a good argument. How about bodily?

- I think you're probably right. He is using body language to communicate his ideas. David thinks that we use our bodily-kinesthetic intelligence all the time. What do the rest of you think?

- Good, I guess if we didn't we would just be blobs on the ground. So you all seem to agree that most things we do require some level of bodily-kinesthetic intelligence. When would there be a time when we would use a lot of bodily-kinesthetic intelligence?

- Right, playing sports, dancing. So it seems to me that what we've discovered is that although we all have all the intelligences available to us all the time, we change how we use them according to what we need to do. Do you all agree?

- When we change what we do according to the situation, we say that the way we are acting is *situational.* So we are saying that the way we use our intelligences is situational. Do you think that even though we all have all of the intelligences we feel differently about how we like to use them?

- Yes, we vary in how strong we feel in the different intelligences. For example, I know that Bill will always use his bodily-kinesthetic intelligence better than I use it because that's a real strength for him. I also know that even though it's not a great strength for me, I use it to some degree all the time. Sometimes I use it quite well when I work out to keep fit, for example. Do any of you feel stronger in some areas?

Let students share what they consider to be their strengths.

- We have also decided that we adapt and change our Smart Profiles according to the situations we find ourselves in and what we need to do in those situations.

Note that *prebeginner* means "I'm not willing to try"; *beginner* means, "This is hard, but I'm willing to try to make it easier"; *strong* means "This is powerful"; *stronger,* "This is more powerful"; and *strongest,* "This is my most powerful."

Situations to Profile

▶ It's conference time at school. You are expected to share information about yourself and your goals for the year and how you plan to achieve those goals.

▶ You had a book report to do. The due date is tomorrow. You are enjoying the book very much, but you went away with your parents for the weekend and didn't get the report done. You want to explain the situation to your teacher and ask for extra time.

▶ You keep score at the basketball game.

▶ You need to get a smaller child from the classroom to the gym.

▶ You and a friend are at the local burger place. You had a burger and fries, no drink. You have been charged for the drink. You want your money back.

▶ Your class is going to the symphony and you will be asked to write a report about the visit.

▶ Someone is picking you up at school. She has asked you to meet her on the west corner at the intersection of two streets.

▶ You very much want to compete in an upcoming intramural track meet.

▶ You have decided to keep a very private daily journal of your thoughts and ideas over the summer.

▶ You are searching the Yellow Pages for computer stores so that you can call and find out where to get the best deal in town.

▶ Two good friends are going to a movie. They haven't asked you, but you very much want to go.

▶ You want to stay up late to see a special TV show. You need to ask a parent how you can trade off the extra time in some way.

- The elevator is out. You need to get up three flights of stairs to reach where you want to be.

- You and a friend are bicycling together. He falls off the bike and cuts his head.

- Your favorite TV show has been rescheduled to make time for another show that doesn't interest you at all. You want to find out when your show is on.

- A friend has asked for a new CD as a birthday present.

- You have decided to develop some kind of organizational system for your desk.

- You need to check on a date that a school project is due.

- You want to get to a friend's house, which is only next door to yours, but there has been an ice storm.

- You join a marching band.

- You enter a drawing contest.

- You want to play the trumpet in the school band. You need to convince the teacher to take you in the band.

- Your parents are out of town. The babysitter has misunderstood directions and wants you to go to bed a half hour before you usually do.

- You must learn all the state capitols for a social studies test.

- You are asked to take a message to the principal's office.

- You are planting a garden.

- You are saving for something you really want.

- There is going to be a party where everyone will bring some food. You have chosen something special that you want to make yourself.

PROFILING A SITUATION

The situation is: _____

_____

_____

_____

The intelligences I need to use to solve this problem are: _____

	Linguistic	Interpersonal	Bodily	Intrapersonal	Spatial	Mathematical	Musical	Logical
Strongest								
Stronger								
Strong								
Beginner								
Prebeginner								

24

Square Pegs, ©1997 Zephyr Press, Tucson, Arizona

••• Activity 3 •••

Empathy and Interpersonal Intelligence

Student Objectives

- To investigate the concept of empathy
- To make the connection between interpersonal intelligence and empathy
- To identify the need for self-understanding (intrapersonal intelligence) before we are able to understand others (interpersonal) and feel empathy

Materials

overhead transparency of student activity sheet 5, Climbing the Empathy Tree
guided questioning 3, What Is Empathy?
student activity sheet 6, Let's Investigate
wall poster 1, Growing to Empathy
overhead projector
blackboard or whiteboard

Teaching the Activity

Project student activity sheet 5, Climbing the Empathy Tree, on the overhead projector. Use guided questioning 3, What Is Empathy? to lead a discussion about the meaning of empathy.

Ask students to identify when and how they have felt empathy for someone. Have them decide which level of empathy they applied in the situation and define how they know that they reached that specific level. Challenge them to identify which intelligences (inter- and intrapersonal) must be applied in order to feel empathy.

Have students work in pairs to complete student activity sheet 6, Let's Investigate. When they have finished, bring the class together to discuss how they completed the activity and why they felt the way they did. Stress the following concept: The reflective nature of intrapersonal intelligence helps us understand others and develop our interpersonal intelligence.

Guided Questioning 3, What Is Empathy?

- Let's think about interpersonal intelligence. Who can remind us what it is?

  Accept definitions and encourage examples. Continue the discussion until you are sure that students understand the concept of interpersonal intelligence.

- What would be a good symbol for interpersonal intelligence?

  Have students draw their symbols on the board or work in pairs to create different symbols.

- How important do you think it is to use our interpersonal intelligence?
- Good answers. It helps us make friends, understand people, get what we need, communicate, and many other things. Let's think more about intrapersonal intelligence. How do we use this intelligence?

- For me, coming up with a symbol to represent intrapersonal is harder. What do you think? Do you have any ideas?

- Now, let me ask you a question that takes a lot of thought because there isn't a yes or no answer. In what ways do you think the interpersonal and intrapersonal intelligences are connected? Is there anything similar about them?

- Good answers. Yes, I agree. If we understand ourselves and how we feel in certain situations, then we are more able to understand how other people may feel in similar situations. Do you think it's true to say that the more we use our intrapersonal intelligence the better we can use our interpersonal intelligence?

- Why do you think that's true?

- I agree again. Understanding ourselves let's us imagine how others may feel. Can we always know how someone else feels?

- Right, we can only guess. But if we understand how we might feel, we are more likely to make a good guess about how someone else feels. Does it help if we have been in the same or similar situations?

- How can that help?

- You are a very perceptive and thoughtful group of people. I would have to agree with you yet again. If we have experienced something we can more easily imagine what someone else may feel in a similar situation. Can we be absolutely sure how someone feels?

- No, we can never be absolutely sure. We can only guess.

- So are we all agreed? To use our interpersonal intelligence well we need to use our intrapersonal intelligence well?

- Okay, now here's another thoughtful question. To use our intrapersonal intelligence well, must we be able to use our interpersonal intelligence well?

  If students answer yes to this question ask them to defend their opinion. Accept their logic and gradually question so that they understand that, although this may be true to some extent, the opposite is more likely. (Always reinforce a student's willingness to state and defend an opinion.)

- Some mixed answers about this. We're not so sure.

- So we agree that although interpersonal intelligence may help with intrapersonal intelligence, using our intrapersonal to develop strong interpersonal is the more powerful. There is a word that describes the ability to feel the way someone else does. It's a difficult word that you may not have heard before.

Write the word *empathy* on the board.

- Does anyone know this word?
- What does it mean?
- Good. It means putting yourself in someone else's shoes or creeping into someone else's skin. Can we really do that?
- No, of course we can't, but we can certainly try. We can use empathy and develop our ability to feel empathy with other people. How?
- Right! Listen, watch, imagine. All good words that help us develop empathy. Why is empathy useful?
- Yes, it helps us understand people, make friends, and care about people.

Put up the transparency of the Empathy Tree.

- Let's look at the different levels of feeling empathy. Who will read the bottom branch on the Empathy Tree?
- Is there any empathy at that level?
- No, there doesn't seem to be much empathy here. Who will read the second branch? Is there any empathy at this level?
- Yes, there definitely is. Do you think this is as far as empathy can go?
- Right, we are only noticing others if the way they feel or act affects us. So it's empathy, but we can go higher. What about the next branch?
- At this level we notice and care what other people feel, even if those feelings are not directly connected with us. So do you agree that there is a big jump to this level? Why?
- Yes, we are stepping outside ourselves. That is a pretty adult thing to be able to do. Let's go to the next level. What's different here?
- Yes, being able to talk with people about how they feel is yet another level. It's more than just noticing. What intelligence would we be adding here?
- Absolutely, linguistic intelligence. Putting words to feelings. What about the next level?
- We usually like to think that people feel the same as we do about things. How is this level of empathy different?
- Very good. It helps us accept that not everyone feels the same as we do. People are different. As you have been looking at the different intelligences you have discovered that people are different and feel differently about things. If someone feels differently from us, does it mean that they are wrong and we are right?
- Again, I agree with you. What's the word that describes being able to accept people who are different?
- Good. *Tolerance.* It's an important idea and at this level we definitely use tolerance. So here we are at the top of the Empathy Tree. Who will read this? It says "We can use other people's opinions to broaden our own feelings and understanding." What's going on if we are able to do this?
- Great, we are learning. So if we get to this level we can really accept that different ideas are okay. If we are able to use all these different levels of empathy, do we always need to stay with the same level?

- No, of course not. We can move around as we want to. The important thing to remember is that we have the choice to move from level to level, up and down the tree. Do you think that it's always easy to move around?
- I don't think so, either. Why not?
- When would it be tempting just to stay down here at the second branch?
- For me it would be very tempting just to stay here if I didn't like the person very much. Maybe I would not want to move if I thought that the person's ideas were awful. Some people can be very persuasive about getting their ideas accepted. For example, what about a politician? Politicians can be very persuasive.

Carry this discussion as far as you choose. It can be a good jumping-off stage for examining the behavior of historical or literary characters.

Climbing the Empathy Tree

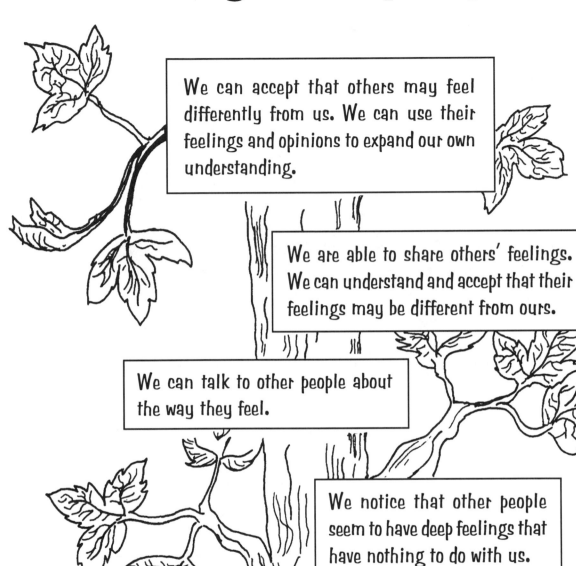

We can accept that others may feel differently from us. We can use their feelings and opinions to expand our own understanding.

We are able to share others' feelings. We can understand and accept that their feelings may be different from ours.

We can talk to other people about the way they feel.

We notice that other people seem to have deep feelings that have nothing to do with us.

We notice how other people feel if the way they feel affects us.

When we listen and look we think only about ourselves and our own world.

Name _____ Date _____

Let's Investigate

In what ways do you think a student and a private investigator are alike?

_____

_____

_____

_____

Your challenge is to investigate the connection between the interpersonal and intrapersonal intelligences.

To start on the trail look up the word *empathy* and circle the synonyms below.

Fellow feeling   **Sympathy**   **Selfishness**

The dictionary will tell you if the word *empathy* is a noun (a person, a place, or a thing) or a verb (a word that tells about an action). By changing the ending we can change the meaning of the word. Fit the word *empathy* into the correct sentence below.

Noun: I felt sorry for the girl. I felt a lot of _____ for her.

Verb: I felt sorry for the girl. I could really _____ with her.

Now put the word *empathy* in your own sentence. Try to tell about a real-life situation where you could *empathize* with someone.

_____

_____

_____

_____

          Square Pegs, ©1997 Zephyr Press, Tucson, Arizona

> **Good investigators have to be good researchers. They need to work through their investigation step by step.**

As an investigator, what intelligence would you use when you organize things step by step?

_____

Next Step

When you feel empathy for someone, what intelligence are you using?

_____

Next Step

> **Before we can use our interpersonal intelligence to understand, care, and feel empathy for someone else, we must try to understand how we might feel in the same situation.**

Which intelligence must you use to imagine feelings?

_____

Can you understand someone else's feelings without trying to understand your own feelings first?

YES   NO

Next Step

Are these statements true or false?

To want to feel empathy with someone we must use our interpersonal intelligence.

True   **False**

To be able to feel empathy with someone we must want to understand how the other person feels.

True   **False**

To understand how another person feels we must use our intrapersonal intelligence to try and put ourselves in the other person's place.

True   **False**

To use our interpersonal intelligence well we must use our intrapersonal intelligence first.

True   **False**

There is no connection between interpersonal intelligence and intrapersonal intelligence.

True   **False**

Intrapersonal
Understanding
ourselves

EMPATHY

Interpersonal
Understanding
other people

Investigators, like researchers, need to write a report to summarize (say in a short way) the results of their investigation. In your very best words, tell how you think empathy makes a connection between the interpersonal and intrapersonal intelligences.

_____

_____

_____

_____

_____

_____

_____

Practice Empathy by Putting Yourself in the Place of Something You Are Not

Put yourself in the place of bird who is trying to build a nest. It is a windy day and it looks as if it might rain soon. You must get the nest finished as soon as possible so that you can use it to lay eggs. What things are happening to make your task difficult, and how do you feel about it all?

_____

_____

_____

_____

_____

_____

_____

You are a racing car. You are about to enter a big race. Your mechanics have worked as hard as they can to meet the deadline, but you know that you are not as well tuned as you would like to be. How do you feel? What will you do?

_____

_____

_____

_____

_____

_____

_____

 Square Pegs, ©1997 Zephyr Press, Tucson, Arizona

Knowing ourselves
(Intrapersonal Intelligence)

Helps us understand other people
(Interpersonal Intelligence)

If we understand ourselves, we can imagine how it feels to be in someone else's place

(Empathy)

Empathy helps us to understand other people even better

(Interpersonal Intelligence)

If we practice understanding other people, we can develop more empathy and develop stronger interpersonal intelligence

••• Activity 4 •••

Multiple Intelligence Posters

Student Objective

■ To create a way to record the different ways each student uses various intelligences

Materials

various colored poster boards
unlined index cards
3-by-3-inch pads of self-stick notes (one pad for each student)
colored markers
glue

Teaching the Activity

Tell students that they will each create a multiple intelligence poster on which they, other students, teachers, and parents will post comments referring to how they have been observed using the various intelligences. Allow students to choose a piece of poster board each in a color that they feel reflects their characters. Have them work on the floor or on large tables to divide their posters into eight sections.

Ask students to draw a symbol or picture on the index cards to represent each intelligence. Ask them to think of original graphics rather than copy something that is already posted in the classroom. Provide all the time they need to complete their artwork to their satisfaction. (Some students may require several sessions to be pleased with their result.) When they have finished, have them glue their graphic card at the top of the appropriate intelligence section.

Designate a section of wall in the classroom large enough to accommodate all the posters. As the posters are completed, have students post them in this area. Provide each student with a pad of 3-by-3-inch self-stick notes. Select one color for student notes and another for teacher and parent notes. Ask students to write at least one multiple intelligence comment about one student in the room and post it on that student's poster (see figure 7 for an example). The only rule is that all comments must be positive. Model for them by making your own notes about each student. Also have students make notes about themselves.

Continue this activity throughout the year. Once a month, have students remove and file their notes in the appropriate section of their classroom portfolios. As notes accumulate, encourage each student to observe in which intelligence notes cluster.

Musical	Linguistic	Mathematical	Bodily
Illustration	Illustration	Illustration	Illustration
self-stick notes / self-stick notes	self-stick notes / self-stick notes	self-stick notes / self-stick notes	self-stick notes / self-stick notes
Interpersonal	**Intrapersonal**	**Spatial**	**Logical**
Illustration	Illustration	Illustration	Illustration
self-stick notes / self-stick notes / self-stick notes	self-stick notes / self-stick notes	self-stick notes / self-stick notes / self-stick notes	self-stick notes

Figure 7. Example of MI posters

••• Activity 5 •••

Developing a Multiple Intelligence Portfolio

Student Objective

- To create a portfolio that
  - ▶ provides a way to categorize ongoing work according to various intelligences
  - ▶ develops critical thinking and self-assessment skills by having students select appropriate work to demonstrate competency and growth

Materials

teacher resource sheet 2, Suggested Documentation Items to Be Included in an Ml Portfolio

student activity sheet 7, My Portfolio Materials Selection Guide

a rectangular plastic file crate for each student

eight hanging file folders for each crate

Teaching the Activity

Explain to students that they are ready to apply their new knowledge about multiple intelligences. Have them label the eight folders with the intelligences. To decorate the cover of each folder, they may draw or cut and paste pictures, or use photographs of themselves to show how the intelligence is used.

Using several pieces of work from each student, conduct a group discussion to decide which intelligence folder is appropriate for each piece of work. Help students understand that some examples can be filed under several intelligences. Reinforce this discovery by telling them that sometimes the lead intelligence of a specific task is very clear and at other times it is not. Suggest that they can explain this confusion when it is appropriate to do so. When you have finished the discussion, hang these folders in the plastic file crates. The size of the crate allows students to store art and craft projects. Give each student several copies of student activity sheet 7, My Portfolio Materials Selection Guide, to help them determine which work samples best represent their abilities and intelligences.

Schedule a regular weekly meeting with each student to discuss rationale for placement of work and to reinforce critical thinking skills. Friday afternoons may be a good time to do this. As the year progresses students' ability to discriminate critically will improve, reducing the need for this meeting. However, we suggest you hold such meetings at least once a month. Structure the system so that students are accountable for maintaining their own portfolios throughout the academic year.

Suggested Documentation Items to be Included in an MI Portfolio

Intrapersonal
- interest inventories
- journal entries
- samples of any self-assessment documents
- recorded or transcribed interviews of personal goals
- samples and suggestions of hobbies or interests
- personal progress charts and graphs
- personal notes on feelings and future plans

Musical
- audiotapes of performances or compositions
- lyrics of songs written by students
- plans and programs of musical performances by students
- musical collages, rhythms, rap, or poetry

Bodily-Kinesthetic
- photos or videotapes of
    - miming
    - acting
    - dancing
    - playing sports
    - doing P.E. activities
    - doing hands-on activities
    - demonstrating

Logical
- write-ups of science experiments
- photos or videotapes of science fairs
- computer programs created or learned
- samples of logical problem solving
- examples of organizational systems

Interpersonal
- feedback from other people (friends, teachers, parents)
- documentation of group project assignments
- letters from others that define the student
- student, parent, teacher conference reports
- community service projects

Spatial
- diagrams, charts, webs, and sketches
- three-dimensional projects
- photos or samples of projects, collages, drawings, paintings
- visual or spacial puzzles solved by students
- videotapes of projects

Linguistic
- drafts of reports
- prewriting notes
- samples of poetry, essays, stories, written by student
- audio- or videotapes of
    - reports
    - debates
    - discussions
    - speeches
    - dramatic readings
- reading or spelling skills checklists or progress reports
- samples of word puzzles

Mathematical
- timed math drills
- samples of best math work
- diagrams or other graphic representations of math concepts

Square Pegs, ©1997 Zephyr Press, Tucson, Arizona

Name: _____ Date: _____

My Portfolio Materials Selection Guide

The topic of this assignment was _____

_____

The subject of this work was _____

_____

_____

I like this work because it shows that I have made specific progress in _____

_____

_____

While doing this assignment I learned _____

_____

_____

To complete this assignment I was required to (check which skills you used)

____ Analyze	____ Forecast	____ Present
____ Brainstorm	____ Generate	____ Put in my own words
____ Classify	____ Identify	____ Question
____ Compare	____ Invent	____ Report
____ Construct	____ Investigate	____ Respond
____ Create	____ Learn	____ Shape
____ Demonstrate	____ List	____ Share
____ Describe	____ Observe	____ Sketch
____ Draft	____ Organize	____ Specify
____ Draw	____ Outline	____ Summarize
____ Edit	____ Perceive	____ Support
____ Explain	____ Photograph	____ Think
____ Express	____ Plan	____ Understand
____ Finish	____ Predict	____ Write

••• **Activity 6** •••

The Conference Portfolio

Student Objectives

- To continue to define the eight intelligences and the ways students are smart
- To engage parents in understanding the concept of multiple intelligences
- To select materials as a focus for explaining the concept of multiple intelligences to parents at student, parent, teacher conferences
- To prepare a conference agenda

Materials

teacher resource sheet 3, Progress Report

student and parent activity sheet 1, Get to Know Yourself

student activity sheet 8, My Smart Profile Rating Scale

student activity sheet 9, My Smart Profile

student and parent activity sheet 2, MI Checklist: What's My Style?

a three-hole binder for each student

page dividers

classroom portfolios

photographs of individual students showing them engaged in activities that demonstrate each intelligence

overhead projector

Teaching the Activity

It is essential that you have students do this activity in a group. You may need to extend the activity over two periods. Make sure that students are comfortable with the concept of multiple intelligences before they complete their own smart profiles. The rating of prebeginner is particularly powerful. Take the opportunity to help students understand that everyone has the choice of rating themselves in this area, but it is important to realize that such a rating means "I won't." Stress that when one moves from a prebeginner to beginner, one has taken a step to "I will try."

Explain to students that it is possible to make a picture or visual representation of how a person may be using the various intelligences at a particular time. Read the My Smart Profile Rating Scale with the class and have them answer the questions individually or in groups. Use their answers to stimulate discussion.

Project the My Smart Profile on an overhead and have students choose a famous celebrity, living or dead, about whom they have some knowledge, for example, Albert Einstein. When they have chosen, work with them to color in the projected profile by defining how they would rate the celebrity. It is usually easier to begin by rating the stronger intelligences first. Emphasize that everyone possesses all the intelligences and may be strong in more than one. As the group discussion evolves, ask students to support their opinions about why they believe the celebrity is strong in particular intelligences.

When the profile is complete, ask students to imagine this person in a situation that represents one of his or her weaker intelligences, for example, Einstein in a dance class. Have them imagine how the profile might change and how the person might need to use some less strong areas to adapt to the situation. Continue to play with the profile in a way that illustrates change and flexibility.

Once you feel that students understand the concept of smart profiling, schedule a quiet time when students may individually prepare their own smart profiles as a culminating activity. Have them file the profile in their portfolios as the first of several they will complete throughout the year. The purpose of profiling several times is to allow students to discover that strengths are relative and constantly changing in a lifelong process.

Students may work as a whole class or in pairs. Give students nine page dividers each. Have them label each of eight dividers with one of the intelligences. Have them label the ninth divider "Reports and Strategies."

Ask students to glue a photograph of themselves engaged in an activity that they feel demonstrates each individual intelligence on the opening page of each section. Have students choose what they consider to be quality work that illustrates their ability in each intelligence to transfer from their classroom portfolios to their conference portfolios. One or two examples are usually enough.

Certain intelligences may not appear to have an example. Tell students that if they look carefully, they may discover that a traditional classroom task unexpectedly illustrates an intelligence. For example, a page of well-organized math may illustrate spatial, linguistic, or logical intelligence. A poem or rap may illustrate musical intelligence because of the rhythm created by the pattern of words.

Most examples will reflect several intelligences. Ask students to decide which intelligence they used most to produce the example. Some examples may be photocopied and inserted into several different categories, which will provide students with the opportunity to explain to their parents that most things we do require the use of all our intelligences to some degree.

Assign student and parent activity sheet 1, Get to Know Yourself, for students to complete as homework before the conference. Have each student use student and parent activity sheet 2, MI Checklist: What's My Style? to complete a more thoughtful smart profile. Explain to them that they are able to do so now as they have spent several weeks learning about themselves.

Help students prepare for the conference. Areas you will need to cover are developing an agenda, practicing their introductions, and deciding on appropriate seating arrangements. If you have a camcorder available, record students rehearsing the process, then allow them to watch themselves to refine their performances. Areas that they may need to practice are greetings, discussion of each work sample, bridging from topic to topic, establishing leadership, and the closing. Students will vary considerably in their ability to do this. Work with every student at the appropriate comfort level. Establish the understanding that all students prepare and lead their conference.

A typical agenda follows:

1. Introductions
2. My test results
3. My different intelligences
4. My work samples
5. My plans
6. Opportunity for questions
7. Closing

You may prefer to present 2, but students need to take responsibility for all other items.

Remember that students have not always been taught how to introduce people. Have students carefully practice this part of the conference and the seating arrangements so that they establish themselves as the leaders at the beginning of the meeting. Starting well will give students confidence to proceed.

Closing on time can also be especially tricky. Help students by discussing the time allowed for each topic and practice phrases such as, "Thank you for coming"; "I hope you enjoyed the conference"; "Do you have any questions before we finish?" Body language such as standing up and holding out a hand is also useful.

Name: _____ Date: _____

Progress Report

	Description Terms			
P	Prebeginner: Unwilling to engage in new learning; unwilling to make mistakes	**S**	Strong:	Developed strengths in this area
		ST	Stronger:	Developed considerable strengths in this area
B	Beginner: Willing to engage in new learning, to make mistakes	**STR**	Strongest:	Greatest strengths in this area

Linguistic
- Oral Communication
- Writing
- Reading
- Participation

Mathematical
- Computation
- Operations
- Concepts
- Participation

Bodily
- Body Awareness and Movement
- Physical
- Physical Fitness
- Bodily-Kinesthetic Communication
- Participation

Spatial
- Patterns and Connection Recognition
- Composition
- Expression of Ideas through Art
- Understanding of Spatial Representation
- Participation

Logical
- Understanding of Questions
- Understanding of Patterns
- Understanding of Relationships
- Reaching Conclusions
- Problem Solving
- Participation

Musical
- Exploration
- Technique
- Auditory Awareness
- Rhythm
- Participation

Others (Interpersonal)
- Respect for Basic Human Rights
- Pattern Recognition and Connection with Other Cultures
- Cooperation with Teachers
- Cooperation with Classmates
- Responsibilities
- Goal Setting
- Respect for Others and Others' Property
- Participation

Self (Intrapersonal)
Intelligences Most Frequently Used
- Linguistic
- Musical
- Logical
- Mathematical
- Spatial
- Bodily
- Self
- Others
- Flexibility
- Participation

Name: _____ Date: _____

Get to Know Yourself

Directions

1. Give each of your parents an MI checklist to complete.

2. By yourself, complete an MI checklist on each parent.

3. Meet with each parent individually and compare your answers with those of your parent by answering the following questions.

How did your checklist compare with the one your parent did?

_____

_____

_____

_____

_____

On how many items did you agree? _____

On how many items did you disagree? _____

List anything you discovered that was a surprise.

_____

_____

_____

_____

4. Help your parents transfer the information from their own checklists to make a Smart Profile Graph.

5. Do the same again with your other parent or any other adult you choose.

 Square Pegs, ©1997 Zephyr Press, Tucson, Arizona

Name _____ Date _____

My Smart Profile Rating Scale

Use these words to draw a picture of yourself.

Prebeginner: "I'm not willing to try.'

Beginner: "This is hard, but I'm willing to try so that I can make it easier."

Strong: "This is powerful."

Stronger: "This is even more powerful."

Strongest: "This is my most powerful."

Remember that My Smart Profile *changes*.

It can change depending on

- **■ time in our lives and time of day**
- **■ how we feel**
- **■ what a situation calls for**

What other reasons can you give for why the profile may change?

_____

_____

_____

Write about one way you would make it change.

_____

_____

_____

Name _____ Date _____

MY SMART PROFILE

	Strongest	Stronger	Strong	Beginner	Prebeginner
Logical					
Musical					
Mathematical					
Spatial					
Intrapersonal					
Bodily					
Interpersonal					
Linguistic					

Name: _____ Date: _____

MI Checklist: What's My Style?

Use this scale to help you discover yourself

1 = not often
2 = frequently
3 = almost always
U = not observed or unknown

Complete the checklist and total the numbers in each column. Use the totals to graph your relative strengths and interests on the smart profile.

Linguistic

Enjoys reading	1	2	3	U
Uses a large vocabulary	1	2	3	U
Enjoys verbal jokes	1	2	3	U
Creates exciting stories	1	2	3	U
Focuses on conversation	1	2	3	U
Enjoys written expression	1	2	3	U
Attends to language	1	2	3	U
Remembers language	1	2	3	U

Total _____

Interpersonal

Likes group process	1	2	3	U
Focuses on interaction	1	2	3	U
Attends to others	1	2	3	U
Makes friends easily	1	2	3	U
Mediates well	1	2	3	U
Helps others	1	2	3	U
Uses interaction with others to relax	1	2	3	U
Collaborates well	1	2	3	U

Total _____

Bodily-Kinesthetic

Plays sports and other physical games well	1	2	3	U
Enjoys movement and dance	1	2	3	U
Likes drama	1	2	3	U
Thinks with body	1	2	3	U
Seeks physical activity	1	2	3	U
Likes to work out	1	2	3	U
Relaxes with physical activity	1	2	3	U
Remembers through touch or movement	1	2	3	U

Total _____

Spatial

Gets around easily	1	2	3	U
Likes playing video games	1	2	3	U
Notices color, line, texture	1	2	3	U

Uses maps and graphs	1	2	3	U
Knows how machines work	1	2	3	U
Remembers images	1	2	3	U
Touches and moves well	1	2	3	U
Likes visual art and photography	1	2	3	U

Total _____

Intrapersonal

Seeks solitude	1	2	3	U
Likes to work alone	1	2	3	U
Knows self well	1	2	3	U
Holds strong personal convictions	1	2	3	U
Values and cares for self	1	2	3	U
Sets examples for others	1	2	3	U
Relaxes alone	1	2	3	U
Models responsibility and independence	1	2	3	U

Total _____

Mathematical

Calculates well	1	2	3	U
Uses math thinking to solve problems	1	2	3	U
Enjoys numbers and number games	1	2	3	U
Understands numerical relationships	1	2	3	U
Likes to transform concrete to abstract	1	2	3	U
Applies math to daily life	1	2	3	U
Uses math to remember	1	2	3	U
Communicates through math	1	2	3	U

Total _____

Musical

Notices music in the environment	1	2	3	U
Enjoys various types of music	1	2	3	U
Likes songs	1	2	3	U
Expresses self musically	1	2	3	U
Feels rhythm	1	2	3	U
Remembers music	1	2	3	U
Uses music to relax	1	2	3	U
Learns through music	1	2	3	U

Total _____

Logical

Likes organized space	1	2	3	U
Approaches tasks in an organized manner	1	2	3	U
Uses systems for learning	1	2	3	U
Likes computers	1	2	3	U
Does science activities well	1	2	3	U
Reasons well	1	2	3	U
Enjoys illogical humor	1	2	3	U
Understands hierarchies	1	2	3	U

Total _____

UNIT 2

Developing Personal Learning Strategies Using Multiple Intelligences

Rationale

It was tempting for us to assume that once a culture of multiple intelligences was established in the classroom and students had identified their individual intelligences, they would use this knowledge in a productive way. However, we knew from experience that this generalization would not happen automatically. We needed to teach it.

Students needed to be guided toward making a connection between understanding how they are smart and developing strategies for learning. If we failed to teach these connections, the new self-knowledge would remain static and therefore be nothing more than interesting.

Our plan was to guide students in a way that would help them develop a personal bank of strategies that capitalized upon strengths and remained flexible enough for students to change and adapt as needed. We knew that with constant awareness and guided practice, these learning strategies would become automatic for our students. Our goal was to guide our students to take another step toward independence.

Student Comment

 Self-profiling is like an autobiography that helps you choose all your tools.

··· **Activity 1** ···

What Is a Strategy?

Student Objectives

- To understand the concept of a learning strategy
- To explore how intelligences can be used to develop strategies

Materials

guided questioning 4, What Is a Strategy?
teacher resource sheet 4, Academic Strategies
student activity sheet 10, Connect Intelligences to Strategies
blackboard or whiteboard
3-by-5-inch index cards

Teaching the Activity

Introduce the concept of learning strategies using guided questioning 4, What Is a Strategy? Have students break into groups or pairs. Using student activity sheet 10, Connect Intelligences to Strategies, as an idea resource list, ask each group to choose one activity and create a "Using Intelligences to Learn School Work" web (see figure 8). Refer to teacher resource sheet 4, Academic Strategies, for examples of how school tasks are related to the various intelligences.

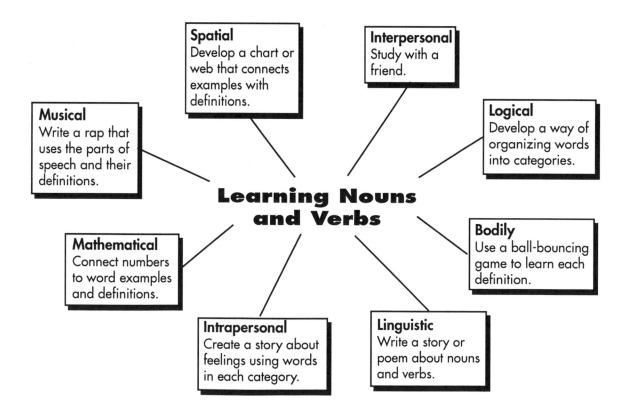

Spatial
Develop a chart or web that connects examples with definitions.

Interpersonal
Study with a friend.

Musical
Write a rap that uses the parts of speech and their definitions.

Logical
Develop a way of organizing words into categories.

Learning Nouns and Verbs

Mathematical
Connect numbers to word examples and definitions.

Bodily
Use a ball-bouncing game to learn each definition.

Intrapersonal
Create a story about feelings using words in each category.

Linguistic
Write a story or poem about nouns and verbs.

Figure 8. Example of a Learning Web

50

Guided Questioning 6, What Is a Strategy?

- We have all been working at understanding the idea of multiple intelligences and deciding which intelligences we like to use. We have discovered that we are pretty typical of any group of people anywhere. In some ways we are like one another and in some ways we are all very different from one another. The important thing we have discovered in looking at different people such as Einstein and Beethoven is that we all have all of the intelligences. Some of us may have more of one intelligence and less of another, but basically, we have them all, and it's up to us when and how we use them. For example, I have discovered [insert something you have discovered about your own intelligences] about myself. What are some of the things each of you has discovered about yourselves?

> **Encourage every student to contribute to the discussion. Stress how intelligence is fluid and changeable. Challenge them to say how they do the following:**
> - ▶ **use different intelligences in different situations**
> - ▶ **change their approaches according to the needs of the moment**
> - ▶ **compensate for less strong areas**
> - ▶ **develop and practice less strong areas**
> - ▶ **build teams by combining strengths**

- It's up to each of us to decide how to change and adapt to different situations.
- So we know a good deal about ourselves. Where do we go next? How can we use what we know? Any ideas?
- You have said that we can use our strengths in ways that help develop areas in which we aren't so strong. How can we do that? How can we improve the areas that are not our strongest areas and make them stronger?
- Good ideas. Using our strengths to develop our weaknesses is a very useful thing to be able to do. Using our strengths is a good strategy. It seems to me that you have already been doing that in many ways. I think we're ready to move on to the next stage.
- First, what do you think would happen if we just said something like, "Well, that was interesting. Now I've learned all this stuff I need to get on with my spelling and math."
- That would be like spending a lot of time cooking a great meal and then throwing it in the trash. Do you think that would be sensible?
- Do you think is would be sensible to spend all the time we've spent learning all this new information and then just forget about it?
- I think it would be a bit of a waste of time also. So how can we use what we've learned? What ideas do you all have about how we can use this information? Think about how we can connect learning something new to something we already know.

- As usual you all have great ideas. I think we all agree it would be pretty silly to spend valuable time learning something and then not use it. I certainly don't have time for that. How about you all?
- You all spend most of your time in school. How could what you've learned help you get better at doing things in school?
- Right, it could be used somehow in school, but how?
- Let's imagine for a moment. Suppose you needed to study for a spelling test. It's important, and you really want to get a good grade on this test, but spelling isn't your strongest subject. You often spend lots of time writing out the words and then when the test comes, you forget where the letters go. Now you have learned something very useful about yourself. While learning about multiple intelligences, you discovered that you are very strong musically. You always knew that you were good at music, but you never realized how strong music and rhythm is for you. How could you use your strong musical intelligence to learn your spelling words for the test?

Use all suggestions to build a web on the board (see figure 9).

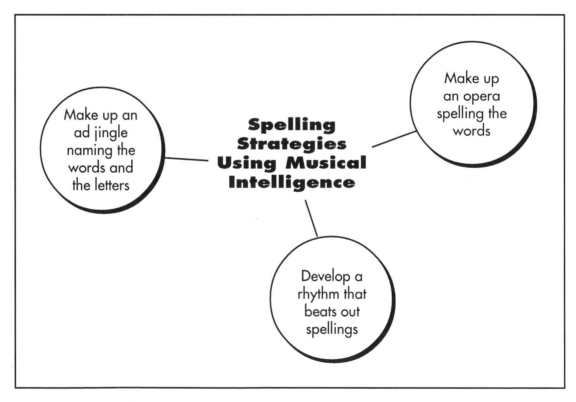

Figure 9. Example of using music strengths to succeed in spelling

- Does anyone know what this word means?

Circle the word *strategies* on the board.

- Let's check the meaning in the dictionary.

Allow appropriate time.

- Many good definitions. When we apply the word *strategy* (for one) or *strategies* (for many) to learning, what do you think we mean?
- Just like the ideas you came up with for using musical intelligence to learn spelling. Every time we develop a plan or a way of doing something, we have used a strategy. Can anyone say why it's useful to have our own learning strategies?
- Do any of you have any strategies that you already use? Any special ways of doing homework or studying for a test or writing a book report. Anything?

Have students share the various ways they have developed to help them learn.

- Many people who work in education have developed all sorts of learning strategies over the years to help people learn various things. We call these strategies *general strategies* because everyone can generally use them to learn. These strategies can be very useful, but the strategies that are really the most useful are those that we call *personal strategies*. What do you think we mean when we use the word *personal*?
- Right, *personal* means individual; specific to each individual. So what do I mean when I say "personal strategies"? Any ideas?
- You are all correct. If I have a personal strategy, it is a strategy that I have developed just for me. I may have taken a general strategy and changed it a bit so it works better for me, or I may have invented one all by myself. I could also have seen the way other people do something, liked their strategy, and tried it myself. Strategies are for inventing, sharing, and changing to make them work as better.
- Okay, let's think about how strategies can be connected to various intelligences. Suppose someone else in the class, who is about to take the dreaded spelling test, is very strong in the bodily-kinesthetic intelligence. What kind of strategies might this person develop to study for the test?

Accept all ideas that students can defend.

- So what do you think are the most important reasons to develop our own strategies?
- Very good reasons. I know that I develop more effective strategies if I have thought about an idea and changed it until it really fits for me. It's like buying a pair of jeans in a store or having Mr. Levi change them just to fit my body perfectly. Does anyone else have a metaphor for changing something to really fit your strengths and solve a particular problem?
- Good ideas.

Intrapersonal
- Write an essay or draw a picture of—
  - My Life to Date
  - My Life in the Future
- Analyze stories to see how the characters feel.
- Write a personal journal.
- Write poems that concentrate on personal feelings.
- Imagine being a character in a play or story and develop a solution to a problem that character is experiencing.

Interpersonal
- As a group, write stories, plays, and poetry.
- Develop topics for class discussion.
- Work as a group or with a partner to develop a project.
- Interview others to find out their opinions on various subjects.
- Work with a partner to drill and practice.
- Work with homework buddy.
- Visit community locations and write about them.

Musical
- Learn Morse Code to practice communication.
- Drill and practice using rhythm—develop rhythm patterns to spell words
- Write a rap to learn poetry, grammar rules, spelling rules.
- Adapt literature to a musical play.

Spatial
- Play word games such as Pictionary.
- Plan and make a video or animated cartoon, essay, story, or project.
- Use magazine pictures, photographs, charts, graphs to create a poster for memory tasks.
- Illustrate a story or poem with drawings that show the sequence of events.
- Develop and act out plays.

Strategies for Language Arts

Bodily
- Play charades to illustrate something to be memorized.
- Act out a dance to remember—
  - vocabulary words
  - story sequence
  - cause and effect
  - predictions
- Develop a ball game to drill and practice—
  - spelling words
  - spelling rules
  - grammar rules

Linguistic
- Write poems, stories, and compositions.
- Brainstorm vocabulary for various topics and file to use as a reference.
- Prepare and deliver a talk.
- Prepare an interview on a specific topic for—
  - classmates
  - school staff
  - community members
- Develop and do cross-word puzzles.

Mathematical
- Define and count different sentence types in a story; graph the results.
- Classify and record affixes to determine those most commonly used.
- Take a class survey of opinions about a variety of literature; tally the results.
- Survey and tally the most common results on spelling tests for each student.
- Record time spent on a topic.

Logical
- Predict what will happen next in a story.
- Develop and organize a system for keeping classroom portfolio up to date.
- Categorize vocabulary words.
- Develop a story grid to record facts in a story.
- Organize time charts.
- Create cause-and-effect chains.

Intrapersonal

- Use visualization to see pictures of the things being studied.
- Draw or write the life story of a scientific phenomenon you are studying.
- Choose a scientific idea and lead the class in an exercise to visualize the concept.

Interpersonal

- In groups, invent and solve science problems.
- Explain to someone outside the group everything you did in a process.
- As a group, research and develop a study process.
- List several attributes that are needed in a good lab partner.
- Work in teams to memorize scientific formulas.

Musical

- Use music to practice biofeedback.
- Listen to music that suggests sounds of the natural world.
- Place a metal plate with sand on the top of a machine or instrument that is playing and observe how vibrations affect the sand.
- Assign musical sounds to various parts of a theory.
- Create jingles to learn formulas.

Spatial

- Draw something you see under the microscope.
- Design a poster showing a scientific topic.
- Do a web or mindscape of something you are studying.

Strategies for Science

Bodily

- Mime a topic you are studying.
- Use chalk to draw diagrams.
- Develop a movement game that acts out something you are studying.
- Use only drawings and diagrams to develop a book of simple experiments for younger children.
- Demonstrate an experiment.

Linguistic

- Choose an internal organ and write a daily journal as that organ.
- Write an adventure story as an element you are studying.
- Be a radio or TV reporter and make a topic being studied into a newscast that explains the concept.
- Write out an experiment so that it can be done by someone who has not done it before.

Mathematical

- Take a survey of habits of teachers, parents, and students; construct a scientific theory based on your findings.
- Take a survey of the number of something you are studying on one street and estimate how many there are in the neighborhood.

Logical

- Study and determine various ways to classify a scientific collection.
- Organize a system to track something you are studying.
- Research past natural disasters such as earthquakes. Look for patterns and try to predict future such disasters.
- Organize a system to record absences due to illness.

Intrapersonal

◆ Study and define the thinking patterns used to solve various math problems.
◆ Develop a chart that bridges math into everyday activities.
◆ Watch and record your mood changes when doing different kinds of math problems.
◆ Create a way of recording math strengths and weaknesses.

Interpersonal

◆ Work in groups to—
  • solve story problems
  • develop problems to practice different operations
◆ Teach a math operation to the class or a younger class.

Musical

◆ Learn math operations using songs, music, and rhythm.
◆ Match different times to math facts.
◆ Develop different raps to learn—
  • multiplication
  • math operations
  • steps for problem solving
◆ Create an jingle to sell the usefulness of math in everyday life.
◆ Chant math facts.

Spatial

◆ Estimate size of classroom, playground, other area, by sight; measure and compare prediction to actual sizes.
◆ Practice math facts using manipulatives.
◆ Use visualization to work through math problems; check against solving problems in traditional way.
◆ Use visual equivalents as comparisons with actual measurements.

Strategies for Math

Bodily

◆ Use various parts of the body as measuring tools.
◆ Design and build a geodesic dome; show math computations you used.
◆ Walk to community locations and calculate distances.
◆ Calculate the space needed for a specific activity.
◆ Develop a chart to record wins, losses, draws in school sports and other activities that result in scores.

Linguistic

◆ Develop a book of story problems for younger students.
◆ Explain how to work a problem while others follow each step.
◆ Use math vocabulary to collect and invent idioms and puns.
◆ Create poems or stories to remember math facts.
◆ Write a story about a trip that requires math to plan.

Mathematical

◆ Learn to use any math tool, such as a calculator, quickly and efficiently.
◆ Do regular, timed math exercises and record the scores to show improvement in accuracy and learning speed.
◆ Record and calculate—
  • weather changes
  • bird migration
◆ Develop a number and letter code to use for interclass communication.

Logical

◆ Develop a filing system to record your math test scores.
◆ Predict, record, and compare scores on planned tests in all subjects.
◆ Develop puzzles and problems to practice changing chaos into order.
◆ Design classification charts that show which operations must be used for which formulas.

Intrapersonal
- Do a PMI (plus, minus, interesting) web of important historical decisions and speculate which intelligences were used.
- Analyze a historical character and one important contribution that person made.
- Choose a panel of important people from various periods and apply their different intelligences to a current problem.

Interpersonal
- Choose characters from various periods and role play a panel to debate current social and political issues.
- Debate the impact of important historical events on today's world and speculate what would have happened if events had been different.
- Choose a historical event and role play a conversation between two important historical figures.

Musical
- Study music written at a certain period and determine how the music reflects the political events.
- Choose a musical period and—
  - make an instrument
  - compose some music that fits the period
- Watch movies about historical events. Analyze the sound tracks, including environmental sounds.

Spatial
- Use clay or papier mâché to create relief maps of countries.
- Develop maps of great historical battles, communities.
- Make flow charts, diagrams, time lines, and webs of discoveries in scientific geographic exploration.
- Imagine the city of the future and draw clothing, housing, transportation.

Strategies for Social Sciences

Bodily
- Act out historical events.
- Organize a specific school or class sports day centered around a particular historical event.
- Play "great moments from the past" charades.
- Improvise available materials to create costumes from the past.

Linguistic
- Choose a historical character and a difficult decision this person had to make and present an argument to support the decision.
- Create a rap that uses historical events and dates.
- Study the poetry and literature of a period and make connections with the political and social environment of the time.

Mathematical
- Create time lines for—
  - important dates in the life of historical characters
  - significant dates of the last one hundred years
- Develop a scale to rate important decisions made by a president.
- Look for patterns in the ages of historical characters at the time they made significant decisions.

Logical
- Research when history seems to repeat itself and decide what events seemed to lead to each repetition.
- Based on the past, try to predict what might happen in the next decade and century.
- Take one century and create a cause-and-effect chain that shows how certain events resulted in other events.

Intrapersonal
- Record how you feel when you—
  - listen to music
  - look at art
  - watch dancing
- Use a mirror to draw your self from various angles.
- Create a mandala journal that records your emotions and feelings.
- Create models and sculptures to show your different moods.
- Use designs and drawings to illustrate various life events.

Interpersonal
- Create a class or group sculpture or mural to represent a specific topic of study.
- Choose a partner and sketch each other from different angles.
- Take a Polaroid picture of self and a friend; create a story mural that incorporates each of you.
- Design and create a mural that illustrates the class personality.

Musical
- Paint as music plays, using shapes and color to reflect the piece.
- Adapt a play or story into a musical show.
- Listen to music and name the various instruments as they are played.
- Create a musical picture by choosing a symbol to represent each instrument; draw the symbol on a grid each time the instrument plays.

Spatial
- Use visual imagery to—
  - imagine and draw a pattern to show the movement in a dance
  - walk inside a painting and imagine how it feels
- Design and draw sets for a play or book.
- Develop a time line that shows when favorite painters were born.
- Use clay to interpret a picture in three dimensions.

Strategies for Fine Art

Bodily
- Create a dance and draw a design of the movements that someone else can follow.
- Use mime to act out certain famous paintings.
- Use finger paint and large newsprint to describe music.
- Choose several composers or artists and make up a playground game that represents them in some way.
- Use musical notes to paint T-shirts.

Linguistic
- Study a painting and write a story about what happened before and after what is depicted in the painting.
- Write a short description of various feelings and moods and paint a picture that represents each description.
- Write poetry about color and mood.
- Take the plot of a favorite book and paint a picture that suggests it in some way.

Mathematical
- Using multiplication tables, develop a geometric design by assigning a pattern to each number.
- Assign a color to each number and use the different numbers on a grid to represent multiplication calculations.
- Create a paint-by-number picture for others to follow.
- Paint a mural that teaches math concepts to younger students.

Logical
- Develop a chronological chart of the life of a painter or sculptor.
- Analyze various artistic and historical periods. Use a Venn diagram to chart which activities are reflected in the music and which are not.
- Choose and research a specific composer or singer. List parallels between significant dates in his or her personal life and the music he or she wrote or performed at the time.

Intrapersonal
- Imagine that you are from a culture different from your own; keep a journal for one week that reflects your life in that culture.
- Describe an ideal climate and research to discover if any site has such a climate.
- Think and write about how you would be different if you had been born in a culture different from your own.
- Keep a daily record of weather around the world.

Interpersonal
- With a group, imagine that you are members of a culture entirely different from your own. Debate how you would perceive today's news.
- Examine a culture different from your own and decide what values are important to that culture. Develop a vocabulary list that reflects those values. Decide how the physical geography and climate have shaped the values of that culture.

Musical
- Study the music and musical instruments used in a culture different from your own.
- Research and sing songs from various cultures.
- Study, explore, or create various rhythmic patterns from various cultures.
- Choose a continent and create a musical pattern by using high notes to represent high land and low notes to represent low land. Use the music in a show.

Spatial
- Study and visualize maps; draw them from memory.
- Investigate various cultures by studying the art of those cultures.
- Use clay or papier mâché to make maps of geological forms.
- Develop a map of the school or neighborhood.
- Transform the classroom into a cultural art gallery.

Strategies for Geography

Bodily
- Learn and perform folk dances and play the movement games of a culture different from your own.
- Research the food of a culture different from yours; take a shopping trip to check the availability of ingredients.
- Study the body language used in a variety of cultures. Develop a mime that uses these gestures and facial expressions.

Linguistic
- Read stories, myths, and poetry from a variety of cultures.
- Develop a vocabulary list of words that reflect concepts that are important to a culture other than your own.
- Check your ability to give good directions: A partner and you use the same road map. The two of you sit back to back. You give your partner directions to a location on the map. See if your partner gets to the correct location.

Mathematical
- Calculate the percentage of a country's population that lives in a capitol city.
- Identify a destination. Determine the mileage from your city. List supplies you would need to make the journey.
- Study the currency of various countries; compare and contrast it to U.S. dollars.

Logical
- Determine a cause-and-effect relationship between geography and major geological events.
- Research and list major events in a country's history and determine how these events shaped the culture of the country.
- Develop a game of "Guess the Culture" using artifacts, current events, and facts from a variety of cultures.

Connect Intelligence-Based Strategies to the Curriculum

Choose several of the activities from the list below and make a web that connects the intelligences you will use to each activity.

____ Learn parts of speech

____ Study for spelling test

____ Read and answer questions

____ Prepare a short research paper

____ Study multiplication tables

____ Study for capitol city test

____ Read a chapter and write a summary

____ Describe one character in the book

____ Study the parts of a sentence (subject and predicate)

____ Say what you know about a triangle

____ Learn a list of dates by heart

____ Correct a paragraph to put in capital letters and periods.

____ Label places on a map

____ Draw a map of the United States that shows your state

Square Pegs, ©1997 Zephyr Press, Tucson, Arizona

••• **Activity 2** •••

Strategies: From General to Personal

Student Objectives

- To categorize and practice strategies used generally
- To adapt general strategies for their own use and to generate strategies that are specific to their own needs and strengths

Materials

guided questioning 5, General Strategies
student activity sheet 11, General Strategies
student activity sheet 12, General Strategies Test Record (3 copies for each student)
blackboard or whiteboard

Teaching the Activity

Strategies are divided into the following categories:

1. Communication
2. Attention
3. Organization

Have students define the strategies within each category and practice using them. Give students copies of activity sheet 11 and use guided questioning 5, General Strategies, to introduce the first category, communication. Once students are comfortable with communication, have them use the activity sheets to practice and record their reactions to the other two strategies. Have students use student activity sheet 12, General Strategies Test Record, to generate their personal strategies in each of the three categories. Encourage students to adapt the general strategies for their own future use.

When they have completed the assignment, have them file their activity sheets in their portfolios for later reference. If possible, have each student start a personal strategy computer file and post strategies in the classroom for reference.

Guided Questioning 5, General Strategies

Give students copies of student activity sheet 11, General Strategies.

- We're going to concentrate on various general strategies. Who can give a definition of the word *strategy*?
- Yes, you really understand the idea of strategies. Can anyone think of a metaphor for a set of personal strategies that we might use to help us learn?
- A tool kit, great metaphor.
- Look at the first page of your handout. Someone give me the name of the category we will be using for our first set of strategies or tools.
- Right. It's *communication*. So this would be building a communication . . . what was our metaphor?
- Right, a communication tool kit, or a communication strategy bank account. Oops! Another metaphor!

- What do we mean by *communication?*
- Does communication always involve words? Right again, not always. For example, look at my face while I say this. (Assume an angry face.) "I am furious." How do I feel?
- Right, pretty mad. Now suppose I just look this way and don't use any words at all. How do I feel?
- Right, still pretty mad. How did you know? I didn't say anything this time.
- Yes, facial expression can communicate a lot about the way we and other people feel. Now, let me give you another example of the way we communicate.

> **Choose a student to tell a story of something that happened that was fun. As the student is talking, show boredom in your body language. For example, you may gaze out the window, tap your feet, yawn.**

- What kind of message am I giving?
- Right, I'm not interested. How am I giving that message? I'm not using words or even facial expressions.
- Right. Body language is very powerful communication. I can tell that you already have some good ideas about this area of communication. Body language and facial expressions are very, very important. Why?
- Yes, they give us extra clues to what a person is trying to say.
- Why do you think we need to set goals for communication?
- Good thinking. What kinds of things could happen if we weren't able to communicate what we need and then understand when other people communicate to us?

> **Lead a brainstorming session about how life would be if people couldn't communicate their ideas and needs to one another.**

- Would you say that it is communication if only one person understands what's going on?
- Right, not at all. Why not?
- I agree, communication is a two way street.
- Let's talk about the kind of communication that goes on in school. For example, what kinds of questions do you ask in school?

> **Possible examples include "How do you work this problem?" "Will you help me?" "May I work in a quiet place?" "When is break (P.E., lunch)?"**

- Good examples. Lots of questions. So let's imagine that I'm in a situation where there are all these words and questions and I'm just not getting all of it. I need the teacher or whoever is trying to communicate with me to repeat something. What are some of the ways I could ask for a repetition?

Possible examples include "Would you repeat that, please?" "I know what you said in the first part, but I didn't get the whole idea." "I heard you but I didn't understand." "I need you to say that again."

- Good. Sometimes just hearing it again will do. At other times that doesn't work. What do I do if I just don't get it after a repetition?
- Right, ask for an explanation. We call that asking for *clarification*. Give me some effective ways of asking for clarification.

Possible examples include "I didn't get it. Please can you say it in a different way?" "I hear your words but I need you to explain what you mean." "I got the first part, but can you say the rest in another way?"

- I'm going to read something to you that I think is quite difficult. I don't expect you to get all the details. I'm not at all sure that I understand everything that the article is talking about. The point of what we are going to do is to give you all an opportunity to practice asking for repetition and clarification.
- Take out student activity sheet 12, General Strategies Test Record, and on the line after the words *General Strategies Test Record for* write *communication*. This sheet will help you try the strategies and record how you felt about each one. This activity will help you discover the kind of strategies that work for you. Don't forget to write in your name and the date. The date will let you look back at a strategy and see how it worked for you at a certain time.
- Look at the first box and call this *strategy 1*; record your impressions. What you are doing is testing this tool to see if it is generally a useful one for you to use.
- Who has finished and can share impressions about communication strategies?
- Good. Go back and look at strategy 2. Another linguistic strategy. Will someone explain this strategy?
- Good. *Paraphrasing* does indeed mean putting things in your own words. Why do you think it's useful to put things in your own words?
- Good, if we can say it in our own words, then we usually understand it.

Choose a passage that students can understand and read it aloud. Proceed as you did with strategy 1, having them complete the box on the second page, following the same process for strategies 3 through 9.

- Let's look at strategy 7. This strategy is really useful and one that some people do easily and others don't think about. It can give a really powerful message to the person with whom we are communicating. Does anyone have any idea what *give free information* means?
- Good ideas. Let me do a little demonstration and you decide which ideas are correct.

- What did you bring for lunch today?
- Okay, you gave me just the facts. Now give me some free information. Some information that I didn't specifically ask for. For example, what kind of jelly and what is your favorite jelly?
- Grape jelly! I really like grape jelly, too. What free information did I get when I asked about your lunch?
- Yes, I learned something about you. I learned that you like grape jelly. I got some free information about you that was interesting. I also like the fact that you made eye contact when we were talking. How do you think that made me feel?

Lead students to identify that it feels good if someone seems to be interested in you.

▶ **Free information gives energy to and expands communication. It makes people think you are interested.**

▶ **Lack of free information limits the communication, makes conversation dull, and makes people feel that you are not interested.**

- How do you think that free information helps the other person?
- Yes, it gives extra information. What is the connection between free information and pleasing a teacher?
- Good. Everyone likes to feel that the person she is speaking to likes to listen to what she has to say. How do you think the listener feels when we give free information?

Go around the class and ask questions and challenge each student to give some free information in her or his answer.

- If we end our free information with a question, what must the person we are talking to do?
- Right, answer our question. Then what happens if that person ends their answer with a question?
- Right again, we must answer. What happens if it goes on like that?
- Yes, we have a conversation.

Have students form pairs and ask each pair to develop and practice a conversation by giving free information. When they are ready, have each pair demonstrate their conversation for the class.

1 Linguistic
Ask a question—request repetitions or clarification when I don't understand something.

2 Linguistic
Paraphrase—restate in my own words what I understood.

3 Linguistic
Talk to myself in my head or out loud.

4 Linguistic
Tape record the conversation.

5 Linguistic and Spatial
Draw or write key word or picture.

General Strategies I Can Use to Communicate

6 Interpersonal and Spatial
Watch what others do.

7 Linguistic
Give free information.

8 Inter- and Intrapersonal
Advocate for myself— say what I need; see teacher; ask others.

9 Interpersonal

Smile!

1 Bodily
Move when I need to without disturbing others.

2 Linguistic
Listen through earphones.

3 Linguistic
Repeat what is said aloud.

4 Bodily
Chew gum.

5 Linguistic and Spatial
Work with cue cards.

6 Interpersonal
Work with a buddy.

7 Linguistic
Tape record something and listen to it again.

General Strategies I Can Use to Get into Focus and Attend

8 Musical
Use a metronome to help you focus on a task.

9 Spatial
Graph progress.

10 Spatial and Logical
Use a highlighter.

11 Spatial and Logical
Mark my place.

12 Bodily
Use a pencil grip.

13 Bodily
Use a special pencil.

14 Spatial
Learn how to see pictures in my head (imagery).

15 Spatial
Draw the lesson.

16 Bodily and Logical
Look away from things that distract me.

17 Spatial
Keep my desk clear.

**1 Logical
and Linguistic**
Use a special notebook
to communicate
daily between
home and school.

3 Logical
Develop my own
strategy forms.

2 Logical
Use a
homework plan.

General Strategies
I Can Use to Get
and Stay Organized

**4 Logical
and Spatial**
Check off
my task sheet as I
complete each task.

**5 Linguistic
and Spatial**
Take notes
or make webs
to remember.

6 Logical
Collect
work samples.

7 Spatial
Develop and
use cue cards.

Name: _____ Date: _____

General Strategies Test Record

General Strategies Test Record for _____

Strategy _____ Using this strategy is _____ _____ _____ because _____ _____ _____ The intelligences used are _____ _____ _____	Strategy _____ Using this strategy is _____ _____ _____ because _____ _____ _____ The intelligences used are _____ _____ _____
Strategy _____ Using this strategy is _____ _____ _____ because _____ _____ _____ The intelligences used are _____ _____ _____	Strategy _____ Using this strategy is _____ _____ _____ because _____ _____ _____ The intelligences used are _____ _____ _____

Square Pegs, ©1997 Zephyr Press, Tucson, Arizona

··· **Activity 3** ···

Using Strategies to Solve Problems

Student Objective

- To generate personal strategies using individual strengths

Materials

teacher resource sheet 5, Communication, Attention, and Organization
student activity sheet 13, My Personal Strategies
problems to solve

Teaching the Activity

Have students break into groups and assign each group one of the strategy categories and a problem to be solved that is specific to their category. Ask students to brainstorm together to generate an appropriate strategy to solve their problem. Have them define which intelligences they used in the process and to give examples of how they used each intelligence.

When they have finished, bring the class together and have them share their information. Make enough copies of student activity sheet 13, My Personal Strategies, so that each student has several sheets. They are to use the sheets for two purposes. Ask them to observe and note strategies the presenting students used to solve their problem. The observing students will recommend additional strategies and intelligences that could have been used, which will benefit the presenters. Then they look the list over to choose new strategies they think they will be able to use.

After each presentation ask students to present their opinions, explain their answers, and offer suggestions for adaptation and ideas to improve each strategy. Have students complete these sheets as they develop personal strategies and file them in their organizational notebook.

Communication, Attention and Organization

Problems to Solve

Communication

▶ You need extra time to complete a project, but your teacher just doesn't seem to understand.

▶ When the teacher uses a lot of words, it helps you to doodle. How can you communicate this to your teacher?

▶ When your best friend is reading, she always scowls and looks worried. This makes you feel that you have done something wrong.

▶ Sometimes your teacher says positive words, but his body language doesn't match the words.

▶ You have forgotten your homework.

▶ You were asked to do a chore at home, but you have extra homework and feel worried that you can't get everything done.

Attention

▶ The music class practices next to your classroom and the noise is distracting. You can't stop the noise.

▶ When you come in from the playground, it seems to take you longer to settle down than it does anyone else.

▶ You find that your teacher has a very dull voice. Every time he starts to talk, your attention drifts off onto something else. You don't want to say anything and offend the teacher.

▶ When there is a lot of activity in the room, you find it very difficult to concentrate.

▶ For the last thirty minutes of the school day, your eyes are constantly drawn to the clock on the wall.

▶ Whenever there is a fire drill, your attention is shot for the rest of the day.

Organization

▶ Try though you may, you always get home without something you need desperately to complete your homework assignment.

▶ Your desk is a disaster. It seems to take you much longer than anyone else to find whatever it is you need.

▶ Getting from one classroom to another on time is a problem. Every time you're late you lose some points.

▶ Sometimes you get home with everything you think you need for your homework just to discover that you don't have the assignment.

▶ Long projects are difficult. You usually leave them to the night before they are due and it's impossible to do a good job.

▶ Your school bag looks as if it contains every work sheet or bit of paper you have used since you started kindergarten.

Name: _____ Date: _____

My
Personal
Strategies
for

UNIT 3

Setting Goals

Rationale

As students began to work on their individual educational plans, the concept of goal setting emerged naturally. We were eager for our students to identify the ability to set goals as a life skill. With the understanding of the ways in which they were smart and the ability to apply this knowledge to develop specific strategies for learning, students were ready to evaluate their future plans with confidence.

The process of accepting or rejecting goals set by teachers, parents, or peers requires several skills. We wanted our students to develop a thinking process that would help determine the worth of such goals. They needed to understand that although this thinking process varies according to individual needs and the demands of different situations, basic questions to address are similar:

- Can I reach this goal?
- How will reaching this goal affect me?
- Will the effect be positive or negative?
- What are the facts I must deal with as I work to reach this goal?
- What are my choices?
- Can I change any of the things that seem to be facts?
- Is it worth my time to try to change these things?
- In what areas am I willing to negotiate?

Developing the process of identifying goals and then defining the sequence of steps required to reach the specific goal is when learning happened. With this system of repeated analysis the process became automatic.

Student Comment

 It's just like learning! You never stop learning so there's always going to be another goal. You never stop setting goals.

··· Activity 1 ···

Setting Personal Goals

Student Objectives
- To develop the ability to define realistic academic and personal goals
- To develop appropriate strategies required to meet goals
- To explore task analysis
- To understand the relationship between cause and effect by taking responsibility for the consequences of personal decisions
- To practice problem-solving techniques and learn to perceive failure as a tool for learning and future planning
- To own and enjoy successful results

Materials
guided questioning 6, What Are Goals?

teacher resource sheet 6, Strategies for Helping Students Reach Goals

student activity sheet 14, Specific or General?

student activity sheet 15, Goal-Setting Interview

student activity sheet 16, Strategies to Reach My Goal

student activity sheet 17, My Goal Plan

blackboard and whiteboard

resources for articles

Consumer Reports for Kids
Mountain Biking
Boy's Life

Teaching the Activity

Introduce the concept using guided questioning 6, What Are Goals? As you work on building the goal web, help students distinguish the difference between goals and strategies. Reinforce the concept that goals and strategies are flexible. A strategy often becomes a smaller goal to help you achieve the big goal. The important thing is not to lose sight of the big goal. For example, if the goal is to improve spelling, then the strategy may be to pay attention to letter order. If the goal is to pay attention to letter order, then the strategy may be to improve concentration when checking spelling. If the goal is to improve concentration, then the strategy may be . . . However, students should never be committed to the second and third goals if they are not the most effective way for them to improve spelling.

Divide class into pairs and give them student activity sheet 14, Specific or General? When they have completed the form, have them share their results and say what they learned about goal setting.

Have the pairs interview each other using student activity sheet 15, Goal-Setting Interview. Have students use the multiple intelligences goals they set in unit 1 to complete student activity sheet 16, Strategies to Reach My Goal. Give students student activity sheet 17, My Goal Plan, and encourage them to link what they know about intelligences and strategies to this goal-setting exercise. Finally, have them take another copy of student activity sheet 15, Goal-Setting Interview, home and interview a parent for homework.

Guided Questioning 6, What Are Goals?

- The weekend is coming up. Who has some interesting plans to share about how you will spend your weekend?

> **Allow students to share their plans, then tell them your plans. State what your goal was when you made these plans, and ask students to share their goals.**

- Bill said he would be having fun. Would you call that a big, general goal or a specific kind of goal?
- I would also call it a big, general goal. I am going to tidy up my garden. One of my goals for that is to get rid of the leaves so that it will be in good shape for planting next spring. My goal is to have a beautiful garden to enjoy next year. Which of those goals do you think is specific and which do you think is general?
- Getting it cleaned up is more specific than wanting a beautiful garden next year. I agree. What do you think would happen to me if I forgot the big goal of working toward a beautiful garden next year and could only concentrate on all the work?
- For me it's really important to remember that big goal. If I don't, then I just feel as if I'm working just to work, and that wouldn't be much fun. What ideas like that do you all have? Think about things you don't like, just as I don't really enjoy raking all those leaves and getting them in bags for the trash.

> **Accept all ideas and have students identify the big goal that is related to the smaller goals.**

- Bill, you don't like doing homework, so why do you do it?
- Because the teacher gives it to you. But does that mean you don't have any choice at all?
- No, I agree. You still have a choice and you choose to do it. Why?
- Because you get into trouble if you don't. So what happens then?

> **Follow the chain back until the student can identify the biggest goal, which, in this case, may be to get a high school diploma and go to college. Reinforce this goal as the big, general goal, and help students understand that losing sight of the big goal gets us stuck with thinking about things that we sometimes don't enjoy. If we lose sight of the big idea, we may get angry and feel cheated.**

- So that big idea is always important even though we often have to break it down into smaller, more specific parts. Here's an example. Let's suppose that you want a wonderful new bike. You would love to be able to ride this bike and show it off to all your friends. It's the only thing you care about. The bike is very expensive and your parents have said that they are prepared to pay for half of it if you will work and earn the other half. Maybe they really can't afford the whole price or they have decided to use this as a lesson in responsibility. Either way, you have used all your powers of persuasion and you know them well enough to know that they are not going to give in on this. What do you do?

Students' answers will vary. Some will choose to give up the bike, while others will choose to earn the money in some way. Accept the idea that everyone is free to make a choice.

- Okay, so Maria has decided to earn the money. How could she do that?
- Good ideas. Basically, get a job. So here's another suppose. Suppose Maria gets a job packing groceries at the supermarket for minimum wage. Everyone pretend to be Maria. You have worked out that it will take two months, eight weeks, to earn enough money for half the bike. It's longer than you want to wait, but in eight weeks you will be cruising around on "the bike." The job starts at 4 p.m., just late enough for you to get there if you go right after school, and it finishes at 7:30 p.m.. By the time you get home, it's 8 o'clock and you still have to do your homework. What's your goal?
- Right, to earn enough money for half of the bike. What happens if you lose sight of that goal?
- Right, you get discouraged and may quit your job. So what do you need to do to hang in there?
- Thinking about the big goal will certainly help. So why is it important to see the big picture, or the forest, and not get all caught up in the trees?
- Yes, when we set goals, it's important that we remind ourselves of where all our work is leading. It's also important to keep on seeing the big picture. What was the first question you had to ask yourself?
- Yes. How would you earn the money? You decided on a job. What then?
- Good, how to get a job. So you kept adding smaller and smaller goals. Your strategy for earning the money was to get a job so that strategy became a goal. You are all very good problem solvers.
- Let's talk about setting goals in school. Here are some very big idea questions. Why do you think the law says that everyone must go to school until a certain age?

Write suggestions on the board.

- What happens if a parent doesn't send a child to school or make sure the child is educated in some other way? Does anyone know?
- You are right. It's not good. The parent gets into a lot of trouble. If the parent doesn't get the child to school, what are the courts likely to do?
- All sorts of unpleasant things can happen. So are we all agreed that we will accept going to school as a given in our society? That means that is just the way it is. It's the law. We can get laws changed, but it would take a lot of time and effort to change this law, and then do you think it will get changed even after all that time and effort?
- Right, probably not. So let's take it as a given, or fact. You all have to be in school until the law says you are old enough to leave. When you do leave school and you are responsible for yourselves, what kinds of things will you need to be able to do?

This question will elicit a variety of responses. Field them as they come and accept that some may sound negative. Try to turn negative ideas into positive ideas whenever possible.

■ Basically, when we are through with school and out in the world at large, we will have to look after ourselves and make our own decisions. Set our own goals and decide how to reach those goals.

Start a web on the board. Your web may evolve a little differently from the example, but try to include similar concepts. Possible leading questions follow:

▶ **What do we need to be able to do to be independent?**

▶ **How can we practice independence skills in school?**

▶ **In what areas can we set our own goals?**

▶ **Whose goals are important to us?**

▶ **Do some of our goals affect the people we care about, such as our parents and teachers?**

▶ **How do we feel if other people are always setting our goals for us?**

▶ **If other people are doing everything for us, are we learning anything?**

▶ **If we want to set our own academic goals, whom can we ask for help?**

Strategies for Helping Students Reach Goals

General Goals

Improve Academically	Be independent	Feel Confident

Specific Goals

Think Positively	Expect Success	Get Help When Needed
Don't Give Up	Be Realistic	Know Whom to Go to for Help
Make Sure the Goal Can Be Reached	Believe in Self	Be Patient
Be Enthusiastic	Work Hard	Persevere

Develop Strategies for Reaching Specific Goals

Square Pegs, ©1997 Zephyr Press, Tucson, Arizona

Name:_____ Date: _____

Specific or General?

Look at these goals and decide which are the big, general goals, and which are the small, specific goals.

| **Going to College** | **Graduating from High School** |
| general or specific | general or specific |

Why? _____
_____
_____
_____

| **Buying a Car** | **Learning to Drive** |
| general or specific | general or specific |

Why? _____
_____
_____
_____

| **Finding a Driving Teacher** | **Learning to Drive** |
| general or specific | general or specific |

Why? _____
_____
_____
_____

| **Getting Homework Done** | **Checking Homework Assignment** |
| general or specific | general or specific |

Why? _____
_____
_____
_____

Name: _____ Date: _____

Goal-Setting Interview

Choose two people to interview.
Ask all the questions below and write down the answers.

1. Tell me an important goal you set for yourself and reached.

   _____

   _____

   _____

2. What made you decide upon that particular goal?

   _____

   _____

   _____

3. What helped you know that you could reach that goal?

   _____

   _____

   _____

4. Often goals are not reached easily. Tell me about the difficulties you faced as you worked to reach your goal.

   _____

   _____

   _____

5. You may have felt discouraged at times. What did you do that helped you work past your discouragement and reach your goal?

   _____

   _____

   _____

6. How did you decide when you needed help, and how did you get the help?

   _____

   _____

   _____

7. How did you feel when you reached your goal?

_____

_____

_____

8. What strategies did you use to reach your goal?

_____

_____

_____

9. In working to reach your goal, what did you learn about setting goals in general?

_____

_____

_____

10. What did you learn about yourself in particular?

_____

_____

_____

For the interviewer

What did you learn about the person you interviewed?

_____

_____

_____

Add at least one interesting thing you learned about yourself while you were conducting this interview.

_____

_____

_____

_____

_____

_____

Name:_____

Date I began to work on this goal: _____   Date I reached this goal: _____

Strategies to Reach My Goal

My big, general goal is

_____

_____

My specific goals for reaching my general goal are

1. _____

2. _____

3. _____

4. _____

5. _____

The purpose of my first specific goal is

_____

_____

_____

_____

The materials that I will need in order to reach this goal are

_____

_____

_____

_____

The number of times each week I will work specifically on reaching my goal are

_____

The time I will spend at each practice session is

_____

Square Pegs, ©1997 Zephyr Press, Tucson, Arizona

I believe I can reach this general goal because

_____

_____

_____

In reaching this general goal I will need

❑ A lot of help   ❑ Some help   ❑ No help

These are the people from whom I can get help if I need it:

_____

_____

_____

This is how I will keep a record to show my progress while I am working toward my general goal:

_____

_____

_____

_____

This is how I will reward myself for success and hard work:

_____

_____

_____

_____

These are some other general goals I have for the future:

_____

_____

_____

_____

Name: _____ Date: _____

My Goal Plan

Strategy:
_____
_____
_____
_____

Intelligence:
_____
_____

Strategy:
_____
_____
_____
_____

Intelligence:
_____
_____

Strategy:
_____
_____
_____
_____

Intelligence:
_____
_____

Strategy:
_____
_____
_____
_____

Intelligence:
_____
_____

My Goal For
_____
_____
Is
_____
_____

Strategy:
_____
_____
_____
_____

Intelligence:
_____
_____

Strategy:
_____
_____
_____
_____

Intelligence:
_____
_____

Strategy:
_____
_____
_____
_____

Intelligence:
_____
_____

Strategy:
_____
_____
_____
_____

Intelligence:
_____
_____

Square Pegs, ©1997 Zephyr Press, Tucson, Arizona

UNIT 4

Practicing Positive Thinking

Rationale

Many students who are unsuccessful in school believe that the things that happen to them are the result of luck or chance. They may reach this conclusion, often unconsciously, through a series of failures that result in the expectation of failure. Repeated failure can be hurtful, and the natural human reaction is to protect oneself from hurt. Through years of observation, we know that a student who has learned to be helpless may appear passive or may develop ways of deflecting hurtful situations. Although these patterns of behavior are understandable, the result is often damaging for the person who is trapped in this cycle of learned helplessness.

The work of Martin Seligman in the area of learned helplessness is an important feature of our approach to teaching. In his most recent work, Seligman (1995) states that research done in 1970 shows that pessimists are more likely to give in to learned helplessness, and that as a result, these individuals are at greater risk for depression. In keeping with his own optimistic manner, Seligman believes that pessimism can be changed to optimism and has provided the documentation to support his theory.

We know that optimistic students are more likely to succeed and that this success results in a feeling of being in control. Our challenge, we believe, is to help our students understand this causal relationship and want to become involved in changing their pessimistic expectations.

Student Comment

When you know about yourself you get that confidence and confidence makes you feel good. If you think you can do it, then you usually find a way.

••• **Activity 1** •••

Optimist or Pessimist?

Student Objectives

- To introduce the concepts of pessimistic and optimistic thinking
- To explore how the way we think affects the way we act and, in turn, may contribute to the kinds of things that happen to us
- To begin to examine cause and affect, personal choice, and accountability

Materials

guided questioning 7, Optimist or Pessimist?

five copies per student of student activity sheet 18, Which Word Where?

student activity sheet 19, Words! Words! Words!

wall poster 2

overhead projector

3-by-5-inch index cards

Teaching the Activity

Tell students that it is important for them to understand the vocabulary that educators use if students are to become part of the planning for their academic future. Introduce the concept of attitude using guided questioning 7, Optimist or Pessimist?

Project student activity sheet 18, Which Word Where? on the overhead projector. Discuss each word and concept with the class.

Divide students into small groups to prepare a mime that illustrates a word they have chosen. Students may prepare the cards. Ask students to share personal situations in which they have experienced the meanings of the words.

Guided Questioning 7, Optimist or Pessimist?

- We've been spending a lot of time learning about and understanding multiple intelligences, looking at ourselves and making smart profiles. We've also been looking at various situations, trying to decide which intelligences they require. You have all developed your own smart profiles, and you're working on your smart profile posters and collecting work samples that show the various intelligences for your portfolios.
- How have you used what you discovered about how you are smart to help you learn? What tool kit have you developed that is very personal and individual to you and helps you learn?
- Right, strategies. Personal learning strategies using your individual strengths. How can you use strengths to make your less strong areas stronger?
- Good examples. I have an example, also. I am strong linguistically and not at all strong bodily. I know I must get exercise to stay healthy, so I started walking. When I first started walking, I listened to books on tape to make it easier. Now I find I just enjoy walking and don't need to listen to the tapes to do it. Does anyone have another example to share?

- Good examples. Once you have learned about the various intelligences, how to use them, and how to develop some personal strategies, you were able to set some personal goals. How did you do that?
- Good strategies. How do you all feel about what you've learned?

Encourage discussion, responding to comments in a way that leads students to identify the fact that understanding themselves makes them feel more confident and better able to make good choices for themselves.

- I'm impressed with how much you've learned and how well you've learned it. How do you think all this understanding can help people build the skills they need to be successful in school?
- How do you think this understanding and these skills can help you in life?
- It's a little like using a computer. If we know how the computer moves around in its programs, then we can use it better. It's really just the same with us. The more we know about how we think and learn, the better we can take care of ourselves.
- There is even more information we can talk about and practice. We have already decided that when we know ourselves well, we feel more confident. When you feel confident, do you expect things to turn out positively or negatively?
- Yes, I think you're right. Things usually do turn out better. I know that when I feel confident I expect to be successful. Sometimes I feel confident when I have thought about the situation first and tried to imagine how it will be. Do any of you ever do that?
- Get ready for something that seems very different. See if you can see how this fits with everything else we have been talking about. Who knows anything about Greek mythology?
- You all know a lot about Greek mythology. Does anyone know the story of Pandora's box?

Wait for response. If anyone knows the story, allow that person to tell the story.

- Well, as I'm talking I'm going to challenge you all again to see if you can see a connection between what we have been talking about and this story. Okay?
- Zeus, who in Greek mythology is the king of the gods, created Pandora, and she was the most beautiful woman you could imagine. She was gorgeous! However, Pandora was not a very nice person and she was a bit silly. Zeus gave her a box and told her that whatever happened she should never open this box. Of course, what do you think she did?
- Right! She opened the box. Out of the box flew all the things that Zeus had put in there, and they were awful. Out came things like greed, vanity, misery, envy. You name any nasty thing and it was there. Pandora was horrified at what she had done and she quickly closed the box, but it was too late. All these awful things were let loose in the world. But Pandora had closed the box just in time to keep inside one very, very important thing, and it is this thing that all human beings have. Some have more than others, but we all have some of this thing. Some of us use it better than others, but we all have it.

Write the word *hope* on the board.

- This is what was left in Pandora's box. Who can give me a definition of this word?
- Good definition. Give me an example of someone who feels hopeful.
- Tell me about some times when you felt particularly hopeful about something.
- Hope is what makes us all do things such as dream, expect good things, try to solve problems, and many other things. How do you think feeling confident is connected to the idea of hope?
- I think you're right. Knowing ourselves helps us feel confident and when we feel confident, we feel hopeful and expect to be successful.

Write the words *pessimist* and *optimist* on the board.

- These are rather long words, and you may not have heard or seen them before. Does anyone have any idea what either word means?

You may either make this into a dictionary exercise or provide the meanings immediately.

- Just as we all have different kinds of minds, we are all different in how easily we are able to expect things to be successful. Some people are just naturally optimistic, while others have to work hard at it. But it's like everything else. If we work hard at something, it becomes easier, then suddenly, it's just the way we think without having to work at it again. We can change pessimistic thoughts into optimistic thoughts. Pretty powerful stuff! Does anyone have any ideas about how to change pessimistic thoughts into optimistic thoughts?
- You are full of ideas. Let's try an experiment.

Pick a student who is strong bodily-kinesthetic and especially good athletically.

- Sally, suppose you don't get picked to play in a basketball game. Would you think to yourself, "I'm no good at basketball. The coach never picks me because I'm rotten at sports"?
- Sally: No
- Why wouldn't you say that to yourself?
- Sally: Because I am good at sports.
- So that pessimistic thought would be wrong?
- Sally: Yes
- But let's suppose you were feeling really low and that thought was the first thought that popped into your head, but you quickly changed your pessimistic thought into an optimistic thought. You might say, "That's not true because . . . "?
- Sally: That's easy. That's not true because I'm good at sports.
- So once you've had that optimistic thought, what might you say to the coach?
- Sally: I'm good at sports, so why didn't you pick me?
- So your optimistic thought makes you act optimistically?
- Sally: Yes.

- Suppose the coach says that he knows you're good but he feels he needs to give someone else who isn't good a chance and you will play next time. Would that explanation help you understand what the coach is feeling?
- Sally: Yes . . . maybe . . . well, sort of. Well, I guess so.
- Okay, we're into words and their meaning sooo . . . before we go any further, we're going to look at some vocabulary that we will be using to communicate our ideas. Some of the words you will know already, so this will just be a review for you, and others may be new words. We're going to use an overhead to look at these activity sheets and work through them together.

Work through the overheads with the group.

Create a mood that invites questions. This time is ideal for you to model optimistic, positive thoughts and problem-solving behaviors. For example, you may tell students "It's okay not to know the answer." "That's a good question, I'm not sure of the answer at this time, but as I refuse to be a prebeginner, I will try and find out and let you know." You may also put the question back to the questioner and the rest of the group: "Good question. What do you think? Anyone else have any ideas?"

When you have discussed the vocabulary overheads, allow students to choose how they would like to work to complete their student activity sheets. They may choose to work in groups, in pairs, or alone. This activity may take one class period, or you may spread it over several days.

When students have completed their packets, continue the guided questioning.

- Okay, so now we have all the vocabulary we need to be able to talk about our new topic. I am going to do a lot of talking at first, so if you have any questions, I want you to put up your hand immediately. If something sounds strange to you or you don't get it, just put up your hand and we can get it straight right away. Are there any questions before we start?
- Here we go with a new topic. The word *resilient*. Who remembers what this word means?

> **Lead discussion to convey that *resilient* means the ability to return to a previous state after stress or change. Use the concrete example of a rubber band to illustrate the abstract concept.**

- What do you thing *resilient* means when we apply it to human beings?

> **Lead discussion to convey that it means being able to problem solve, recover from adversity, and use mistakes to learn.**

- Why is it important for human beings to be resilient?
- Yes, if we couldn't be resilient, maybe we wouldn't learn all sorts of things. We must be able to fail sometimes. If we're resilient, we can bounce back, just like a sling shot, and try again.
- What kind of person is going to be more resilient, an optimistic person or a pessimistic person?

- Yes, an optimist. Another reason that thinking optimistically is better than thinking pessimistically. People who feel helpless feel that there is nothing they can do to change what happens to them. They seem to feel that what happens is just luck and that they can't change their luck. What do you think?
- If people feel in control, they feel that the things that happen to them usually happen because of something they have done. For example, if you didn't study for a spelling test and failed it, how would you feel?
- Who was in control of what happened to you?
- Right, you would be in control because you had made a choice not to study. So could you feel optimistic about another test after you have learned that you must study first?
- We're right back to the Pandora story. Does hope make people feel pessimistic or optimistic?
- Right again. Optimistic.
- We are going to take a close look at the different things that make people feel optimistic. For a start, we know that we are constantly carrying on a conversation with ourselves in our heads. This conversation is called *automatic thinking*. Most of the time, this thinking is happening so quickly that we don't even know that it's happening. But these automatic thoughts are very important because they affect how we feel. So the way we think affects the way we feel.
- In turn, our feelings affect the way we act, which, again, affects what happens to us. It's all rather like an endless chain that goes on and on.

Draw four interlocking circles on the board (see figure 10).

- If the first thing in the chain is a problem, what do you think happens next in the chain?

Write the word *problem* in the first circle.

- Good, we react to that problem and we have some fast thoughts about the problem.

Write the word *thoughts* in the second circle.

- So what comes after our thoughts?
- Yes, our thoughts make us feel a certain way.

Write the word *feelings* in the third circle.

- So this one is tricky. What do you think we do after we have had thoughts and feelings?
- Right, we do something. We act.

Write the word *actions* in the fourth circle.

- How do we act if our thoughts are negative and pessimistic?
- Yes, we tend to act negatively. Now here is a problem. If our pessimistic thoughts came quickly and impulsively, what can we do to change our pessimistic thoughts to optimistic thoughts?

90

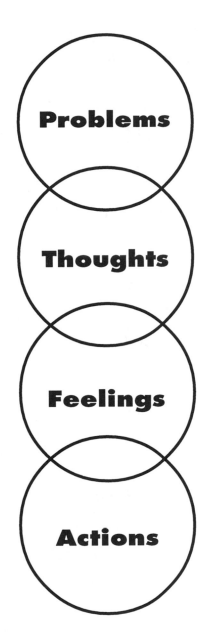

Figure 10. Problems to actions

- Good thinking. We can go back and change our pessimistic thoughts to optimistic thoughts. It's not always easy, but over the next weeks, we're going to practice changing pessimistic thoughts to optimistic thoughts. And, if we have more optimistic thoughts, how are we more likely to feel?

- You all have the idea.

    Refer to the problem, thoughts, feelings, actions circles.

- The way we think affects the way we feel and the way we feel affects the way we act and finally the way we act often affects what happens to us. And . . . there is really good news—we can control the way we act. But what must we change first?

- Right, the way we feel, and what must we change to change the way we feel?

- Right again. Our thoughts. The way we think.

Name: _____ Date: _____

Look in the word box. Write the correct word under the correct picture.

Name: _____ Date: _____

Look in the word box. Write the correct word under the correct picture.

4

5

Word Box

1	**Optimism**	**Pessimism**
2	**General**	**Specific**
3	**Personal**	**Impersonal**
4	**Permanent**	**Temporary**
5	**Positive**	**Negative**

Name: _____ Date: _____

WORDS! WORDS! WORDS!

Resiliency
Impulsivity
Adversity

Resiliency means _____

_____

_____

Impulsivity means _____

_____

_____

Adversity means _____

_____

_____

Put each word into a sentence in a way that gives a good idea of what the word means.

1. _____

_____

_____

2. _____

_____

_____

3. _____

_____

_____

Square Pegs, ©1997 Zephyr Press, Tucson, Arizona

The Optimistic Thinking Chain

The way
we think

Affects
the way
we feel

The way
we feel

Affects
the way
we act.

The way
we act

Affects
what
happens
to us

THINKS

Right! My thought about this made me feel fine. Now what do I do?

95

<h1>••• Activity 2 •••</h1>

Thoughts before Feelings

Student Objectives

- To understand that pessimistic thinking is often impulsive and incorrect and can be changed with optimistic inner language
- To become aware of and begin to monitor inner language
- To examine the concepts of permanent versus temporary situations
- To begin to take responsibility for personal choices and accept accountability for results

Materials

guided questioning 8, Optimistic Self-Talk
student activity sheet 20, Thoughts before Feelings
student activity sheet 21, Change the Outcome
overhead projector
a selection of overhead transparencies of student activity sheet 24
art materials

Teaching the Activity

Introduce the concept of inner language using guided questioning 8, Optimistic Self-Talk, and demonstrate the difference between permanent and temporary situations. Project on an overhead projector transparencies of student activity sheet 20, Thoughts before Feelings, and discuss the idea that our thoughts produce feelings, that these feelings may be angry, sad, or happy. Help students decide if each situation is permanent or temporary.

Make enough copies of student activity sheet 21, Change the Feelings, to allow students to work in pairs or small groups. Students will change the thoughts box to produce each of the three different feelings.

After students have completed the student activity sheet, bring the class together and ask each pair or group to act out a skit that illustrates how they arrived at the three different outcomes.

Guided Questioning 8, Optimistic Self-Talk

- We have already done some talking about thinking optimistically. What do we mean when we say that everyone talks to themselves?
- Right, it's what goes on in our heads most of the time. Do we ever talk to ourselves out loud?
- Yes, sometimes thinking out loud is a good strategy that everyone uses. Do you remember that word *impulsive?* What does it mean?
- Yes, it means doing things very quickly, sometimes without thinking or after thinking too fast. Sometimes when something goes wrong, my first fast thought may be something like, "This is a bad day; nothing ever goes right for me." Does this sometimes happen to any of you?

- I think it happens to everyone sometimes. But I find that if I choose not to go with my first impulsive thought, I can change what I think to something like, "I'm not having a good day today. Never mind. It's just today. Most days are good. Tomorrow will be better." Which is optimistic, the first thought or the second thought?

- Certainly the second one is much more optimistic. How do you think I would feel after I had the first thought?

- That nothing's going right for me. Would I feel crummy or okay?

- Pretty crummy right? How do you think that feeling would make me act, okay or bad tempered?

- When we feel crummy we tend to act crummy. Think for a minute about my second thought. That most days are pretty good. Tomorrow will be better. How do you think I would feel after that thought?

- I agree, not nearly so crummy. So how would I act after that feeling?

- I agree with you. I probably wouldn't be nearly so upset. In fact, I think I would feel okay. So I could move on and act as if things are okay. Not great, but okay. There's something else very important about my second thought. Do you remember the vocabulary we worked with? The two words I'm interested in here are *permanent* and *temporary*. Does anyone remember what these words mean? Remember the green hair?

- Right, *temporary* means "not forever." Just as his hair wouldn't stay green forever. *Permanent* means "forever." Can you give me some examples of things that are permanent?

- Good examples. So was my second thought temporary or permanent, and how do you think I felt after that thought?

- Temporary. So I felt, okay, today's not great but most days are fine and some are even terrific, so this situation won't last forever. Do you think that made me feel better or worse?

- Of course. Silly question. Much better. What about my first thought? Poor me, nothing ever goes right for me. Is that true?

- Of course not. My first thought was just not true because most days are pretty good. What a shame if I get totally stuck with that first thought and feel and act badly for the rest of the day!

- Here's another question. What would happen to me if I really got stuck in that way of thinking? How would I feel about myself?

- It would be pretty depressing. But it can happen. The really good news is something we have already learned: we all have some control over the way we think. It's often not easy, especially when we are sad or upset, but we can get something positive and optimistic out of every situation if we choose to. Who do you think has most control over the way you think?

- Yes, without a doubt, you do. I may decide to listen to something Nick says and I might like his idea and decide that I want to think that way, too. But I have made the choice to listen to, think about, and accept what he says. It's all my choice. Nobody can tell me how to think. I can be a pessimistic thinker or an optimistic thinker; it's up to me. Do you think people are different regarding how easily they think one way or the other?

- Yes. Just as we all have different kinds of minds, some of us are more naturally optimistic or pessimistic. That's just the way we are. Psychologists and other people who study how we talk to ourselves and feel about ourselves have discovered that people who tend to be naturally more pessimistic can change if they want to and become optimistic, and optimistic people are generally happier and more successful in life.
- So . . . why do you think we are going to practice optimistic thinking?
- Yes, it's another way of taking control of our lives and the things that happen to us.

Name: _____ Date: _____

Thoughts before Feelings

1. Record responses that will evoke each of the different feelings.

Problem

Thoughts

Feelings

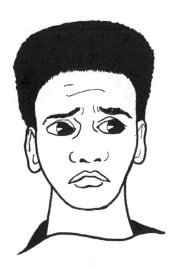  

ANGRY   **NOT OK**   **OK**

Name:_____ Date:_____

Thoughts before Feelings

1. Record responses that will evoke each of the different feelings.

Problem   **Thoughts**

Feelings

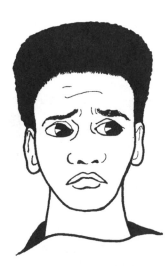

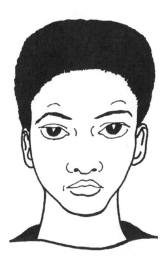

ANGRY   **NOT OK**   **OK**

Name: _____ Date: _____

Change the Feelings

1. Record responses that will evoke each of the different feelings.

Problem

Thoughts

Feelings

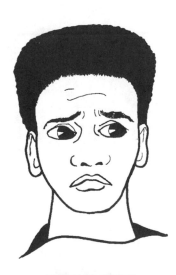

ANGRY

NOT OK

OK

Name:_____ Date:_____

Change the Feelings

1. Record responses that will evoke each of the different feelings.

Problem

Thoughts

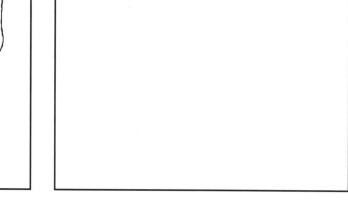

Feelings

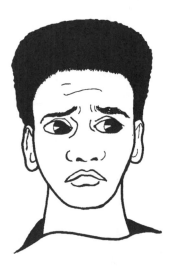

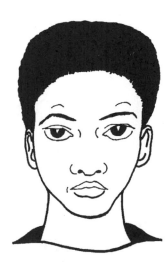

ANGRY   **NOT OK**   **OK**

Name: _____ Date: _____

Change the Feelings

1. Record responses that will evoke each of the different feelings.

Problem

Thoughts

Feelings

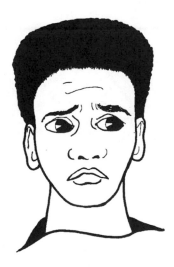

ANGRY

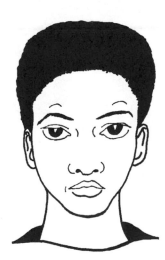

NOT OK

OK

Name:_____ Date: _____

Change the Feelings

1. Record responses that will evoke each of the different feelings.

Problem

Thoughts

Feelings

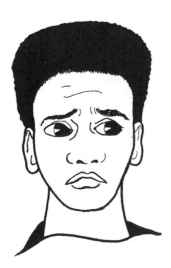

ANGRY

NOT OK

OK

••• Activity 3 •••

That's Not True Because . . .

Student Objective

■ To continue to build automatic optimistic thinking by identifying and changing pessimistic thoughts to optimistic thoughts

Materials

student activity sheet 22, That's Not True Because . . .
student activity sheet 23, Situation Cards

Teaching the Activity

Have students work independently or in groups to complete student activity sheet 22, That's Not True Because . . ., to reflect on changing pessimistic thinking. Bring the class together to share and discuss the situations you assign them. Run copies of student activity sheet 23, Situation Cards, on card stock and cut each page into cards to form a deck. Students may do this.

Have students take turns drawing a card, reading the situation, saying, "That's not true because . . . ," and providing the reason. Each situation is open for discussion.

Remind students that not all impulsive thoughts are pessimistic. What you are working to do is to help them make their brains more likely to think optimistically when they think automatically. Explain to students that doctors who have been studying the brain know that we can actually change how our brain works if we work hard enough. Tell students that the secret to changing our brains is the secret to learning anything new: We must decide what we are going to do and stick with it, which is why they will be doing lots of activities about optimistic thinking.

Remind them how the brain makes connections and grows dendrites. You may choose to use the following metaphor to explain how consistency and repetition can put something into the brain:

Many years ago, a boy and his sister walked to school together every day. One day the girl suggested that they take a shortcut across a field. The boy didn't want to go that way at first because the grass in the field scratched his legs. His sister assured him that, if they went that way often enough, they would tread down all the grass and wear a path. The boy agreed.

The first time they took the shortcut, they left hardly any kind of path at all, but after about a month of walking the same way across the field twice on every school day, the grass was beaten down and there was a path. The girl and her brother walked this way for the rest of that year and, indeed, for the rest of their schools days. By the time the girl graduated, all the grass had worn away and the path was there forever.

Getting things into our memory is exactly the same. The more we repeat something, the more it wears a path in our memory.

Explain that the need to be consistent is the reason that some phrases are repeated over and over. One such phrase will be, "That pessimistic thought is not true because . . ."

Name: _____ Date: _____

That's Not True
Because . . .

Write about two situations that have happened to you in the past or may happen to you in the future about which your automatic thinking has been or may be pessimistic. Use the "That's Not True Because . . . " phrase to come up with more optimistic reactions.

Situation 1

_____

_____

_____

_____

That's Not True Because . . .

_____

_____

_____

_____

Situation 2

_____

_____

_____

_____

That's Not True Because . . .

_____

_____

_____

_____

Student Activity Sheet 23, Situation Cards

Situation
Kathy loves her class and works hard. She thinks that Ms. Smith is the best teacher she has ever had. It's almost Christmas and for the first time, Kathy forgets to bring in her homework.

Thought
I'm so stupid. Now Ms. Smith will hate me.

That's Not True Because . . .

Situation
Joe uses the library in his neighborhood. They usually have, or are able to get, the books he needs. On one day, he needs a particular book and the librarian has told him it's not available.

Thought
That library is no good.

That's Not True Because . . .

Situation
Steve generally does well on timed math drills, and he's proud of his consistently good scores. Today his mind is on buying skates after school. His score drops dramatically.

Thought
How could I let this happen? I'm stupid.

That's Not True Because . . .

Situation
Jason wants season tickets for his local basketball team. By the time he gets around to getting them they are all gone.

Thought
Just my luck; I always have bad luck.

That's Not True Because . . .

Situation
Charlie has always had difficulty reading. He has recently been diagnosed with a reading disability. His parents have hired a tutor, but after a week his reading is no better.

Thought
I just can't read and I'll never get better.

That's Not True Because . . .

Situation
Jennie's husband is usually good at going to the store on his way home from work. She has forgotten to get milk and calls his office to ask him to pick some up on his way home. He says no, he's too busy.

Thought
He never does anything.

That's Not True Because . . .

Situation
Greg has always been a big star on the baseball team. Lately a lot of his time has been spent preparing for a lead part in the school play in which he was a great success. When baseball season starts, he doesn't make the team.

Thought
The coach isn't fair.

That's Not True Because . . .

Situation
Paul is a good actor and usually gets the lead. This year the school is doing a musical and another boy has a better voice, but isn't nearly as good an actor. The other boy gets the part.

Thought
I always knew I wasn't lead material.

That's Not True Because . . .

Situation

Sandy is a good cook. Friends love to come to her house for supper. Something very strange happens to a cake she is baking for dessert for a big supper. The cake looks good, but tastes awful.

Thought

My reputation as a good cook is completely ruined forever.

That's Not True Because . . .

Situation

Jennifer is good at planning and she loves that her friends often ask her to plan outings. She has organized a picnic, but she wakes up to awful thunderstorms on that day.

Thought

I'm so unlucky. The weather is always letting me down.

That's Not True Because . . .

Situation

Janet has a few special friends. They usually sit together at lunch time, but today all her friends are sitting with other girls in the class.

Thought

They don't like me any more.

That's Not True Because . . .

Situation

Patrick swims well but he decides he wants to take diving lessons. It's hard, but Patrick makes his first dive from the side of the pool. The coach doesn't give Patrick a lot of feedback about how he did on that dive.

Thought

Well, that was a disaster. The coach didn't say a word. I'll never learn.

That's Not True Because . . .

Situation

Debbie loves the way her children rush to eat her freshly baked cookies when they get in from school. Today they are in a hurry to meet a friend and don't even notice the cookies.

Thought

They don't care at all that I make cookies every day for them.

That's Not True Because . . .

Situation

Jamie is a good student, but he has a real problem with organization. He is very motivated to get a system going that he thinks will get him from being a straight *B* student to being a straight *A* student. Nothing he tries seems to work.

Thought

It's no good; I'm just hopeless.

That's Not True Because . . .

Situation

David thinks Mr. Jones is a good teacher and usually fair, but today he is doing nothing but complaining and seems to be picking on everyone.

Thought

Why is he picking on me? He is always accusing me of something I haven't done.

That's Not True Because . . .

Situation

Danny likes to do his written homework assignments on his good old reliable word processor. He comes home excited about a story he has to write. His computer is down.

Thought

That computer is rotten; it never works.

That's Not True Because . . .

Square Pegs, ©1997 Zephyr Press, Tucson, Arizona

Situation
Tammy teaches first grade. She loves the kids in her class and knows that she is a good teacher. It's report time and it seems that she spends all her time at work, writing and preparing reports for meetings.

Thought
I'll never have time to do anything but paperwork again.

That's Not True Because . . .

Situation
George is a great speaker. He is funny and entertaining. People love to come and hear his talks. He has a bad cold and feels awful, but he needs to go ahead with a scheduled speech. It turns out to be dull and the audience looks bored.

Thought
I've lost my touch.

That's Not True Because . . .

Situation
Bill's car is old, but he takes good care of it and it runs well. He is proud when people comment on how good it looks and how well it runs. Today he has an important appointment and the car won't start.

Thought
This lousy car. It's no good at all.

That's Not True Because . . .

Situation
Julie leaves her new jacket in the playground. The teacher won't let her go and get it until the class is over. When she goes to the playground to look for it after school, it's gone.

Thought
It's all that lousy teacher's fault if my jacket has been stolen.

That's Not True Because . . .

Situation
Jeff usually spends Sundays with his father. They do fun things together. This Sunday, his Dad tells Jeff he can't make it because he has to work.

Thought
So that's that. He just doesn't want to spend Sundays with me anymore.

That's Not True Because . . .

Situation
Cassy and Janie are best friends and everyone says that they are both popular, but Janie seems to get more dates than Cassy.

Thought
Janie gets all the guys. I must be a real dog.

That's Not True Because . . .

Situation
Cliff likes his job much better than he likes his boss, Mr. Green. Cliff stays out of Mr. Green's way and does his job well. Mr. Green is leaving and a new person is coming.

Thought
I bet this new guy will think I'm a creep, too.

That's Not True Because . . .

Situation
Greg likes to take his lucky pencil to exams or tests. Today he has a big math exam. Math is his best subject; in fact, someone once called him a math whiz. He forgets that lucky pencil.

Thought
That's it. No pencil, no luck. I'm going to fail.

That's Not True Because . . .

Situation
Sam is a terrific skier. He loves the feeling of being in control as he speeds down a difficult run with confidence. He enters a race and feels let down when he comes in sixth in a field of ten.

Thought
I'm not that good. Maybe I should just give up skiing.

That's Not True Because . . .

Situation
At Kay's birthday party her friends go off into a corner and start whispering.

Thought
Bunch of jerks. It's my party and they're talking about me and leaving me out.

That's Not True Because . . .

Situation
Connie gets called to the front of the class to work on the board to solve a math problem. She hasn't studied and can't do it. She is usually a star in math.

Thought
That teacher really doesn't like me and now everyone will think I'm a fool.

That's Not True Because . . .

Situation
Betty, Jane, and Cary have been friends since kindergarten. Lately, Betty has been acting strangely to Cary, but Jane seems fine. Betty tells Cary that she and Jane don't like her any more.

Thought
Betty and Jane hate me.

That's Not True Because . . .

Situation
Every Saturday, Peter takes Susan to the movies. Last Saturday, they had a big argument about the movie. He calls her on Wednesday to say he will be busy the coming Saturday but will see her next week.

Thought
That's it! He's sick of me.

That's Not True Because . . .

Situation
Ann often records her favorite TV show to watch after she has done all her homework. The last episode is coming up and she sets the recorder carefully. When she settles down later to watch it, there is nothing on the tape.

Thought
I am just the unluckiest person in the world. Why do these things happen to me?

That's Not True Because . . .

Situation
Bobby is a fantastic artist; everyone says so. He enters a national art show and is disappointed when he gets only an *honorable mention*.

Thought
Why has everyone been telling me how good I am when I can't even come in third in a dumb show? I'm no good at all.

That's Not True Because . . .

Situation
Ginger is asked to speak on television. She is very excited, but when the cameras roll, she dries up and can only stumble through what she plans to say.

Thought
That's it. Everyone in the world saw me make a fool of myself.

That's Not True Because . . .

Situation
Jenny babysits for the Smiths. Mrs. Smith likes her to take the children to the local playground. Jenny is responsible and takes good care of them. Six-year-old Michael falls and cuts his knee.

Thought
They will never forgive me for this. I shouldn't have taken them to the playground.

That's Not True Because . . .

Situation
Steven is careful with his money and has a growing bank account. He decides to invest a small amount, but unfortunately the investment fails and he loses the money he invested.

Thought
Oh, boy! What an idiot. I should never invest again; I will never understand how to do it.

That's Not True Because . . .

Situation
Janet loves to travel and does so whenever possible. Last year she was in four different countries. She has been working hard and feels tired and fed up. Her next vacation time is two months away.

Thought
I never get to go anywhere.

That's Not True Because . . .

Situation
James is late for an appointment. He drives at 60 miles an hour in a 45-mile-an-hour zone. He gets pulled over by a traffic cop who issues him a ticket.

Thought
Boy, that cop must have had a bad day and was just looking for someone to give a ticket to.

That's Not True Because . . .

Situation
Sally is a big movie fan and goes often. She has been looking forward to seeing a particular movie, but is very busy at work. By the time she has time to go, the movie has gone and won't be on video for months.

Thought
I am always working. I never get to do anything else.

That's Not True Because . . .

Situation
Jane usually takes her shower in the morning. She likes to get up early before anyone else is awake and enjoy the quiet house. She accidentally oversleeps and wakes in a panic.

Thought
Oh, boy! My whole day is ruined.

That's Not True Because . . .

Situation
Christine's mother usually picks her up at school. Today she calls to ask Christine to take the bus home, saying she will explain why later.

Thought
I bet she's doing something for my brother. She never bothers about me.

That's Not True Because . . .

Situation
Julie has always taken her vacation at the same place. This year she decides to go somewhere different. She doesn't like the new place nearly as much and doesn't have a very good time.

Thought
I should never change anything.

That's Not True Because . . .

<h1 align="center">••• Activity 4 •••</h1>

Good-Bye to "I Can't"

Student Objectives

- To develop a personal list of activities that students believe they can not do well
- To remove the phrase "I can't" from vocabulary
- To decide in which areas they are willing to move from prebeginner and discard the "I won't" phrase
- To understand the difference between "I can't" and "I won't"

Materials

guided questioning 9, Removing "I Can't"

student activity sheet 24, Let's Get Rid of "I Can't"

blackboard or whiteboard

shoe box

paper

ribbon

paper doilies for decoration

weatherproof clay

audiotape with "I'm a Cock-Eyed Optimist" from *South Pacific*

Teaching the Activity

Introduce the concept of the impact of saying "I can't" using guided questioning 9, Removing "I Can't." Lead students to discover how prebeginner on the Smart Profile Rating Scale is related to the two phrases "I can't" and "I won't." For example, a prebeginner makes the choice to say, "I am not willing to try." He does not mean, "I can't" but "I won't." Help students understand that "I won't" is prebeginner while "I will try" is beginner.

Join students in listing the various activities that they usually say "I can't" about. For example, "I can't sing." "I can't get organized." Allow students to share any personal "I can't" phrases they frequently say and to lead the class in brainstorming for negative words that are often attached to "I can't."

Give students student activity sheet 24, Let's Get Rid of "I Can't." When they have completed it, have them cut up their lists so that each "I can't" may be folded separately and placed in the casket. In small groups or as a class, assign various tasks related to the funeral ceremony. For example, someone will write an appropriate litany, someone else will dig a hole, preferably close enough to the classroom for it to be seen easily through a window. Some will make a tombstone, and others will decorate the casket. Some will prepare the schedule for the events of the funeral, and others will prepare the refreshments for the wake. Encourage all students to contribute to the litany so that everyone will have a part to read.

Determine a suitable time for the funeral ceremony. Invite parents and other teachers to attend. Everyone may dress in black and behave in a suitably solemn manner.

Guided Questioning 9, Removing "I Can't"

- Who sometimes says "I can't"?
- Almost everyone says "I can't" at one time or another. I often find I say it when I really don't mean it at all. Let me give you an example. Sometimes I might say something like, "I can't clean off my desk. I just don't feel like it." Is it really that I can't do it?
- You are right. Sometimes I do it. So I can do it. So what am I really saying if I just don't feel like doing something that I can do?
- Yes, I am really saying, "I won't." It isn't that I can't at all. There is a big difference between the words "I won't" and the words "I can't." Give me some examples of things that you really can't do.

> **Write responses on the board. If students supply activities that they can do, challenge them to define the difference between "I can't" and "I won't" again.**

- How do you think these two phrases are like *beginner* and *prebeginner*?
- If we choose to be a prebeginner are we saying "I can't" or "I won't"?
- I agree. "I won't" is really being a prebeginner and sometimes we use "I can't" when we really mean "I won't." Do you think "I can't" is a negative or a positive statement?
- If "I can't" is negative, how can we make it positive?
- Right, "I can" is the positive. Which phrase would a pessimist use, "I can" or "I can't?"
- "I can't" is definitely pessimistic. So what is optimistic?
- Great, "I can" is definitely more optimistic. How about "I won't?"
- Yes, very pessimistic. So what would be optimistic?
- Good, "I will" is definitely more optimistic. So I would have to say, "I can clean my desk, but I won't." Sometimes we just don't feel like doing something. If that's what we decide, then it's okay to say "I won't," just as long as we realize that it isn't that we can't do it, it's that we don't choose to do it. When can we use the phrase "I can't" appropriately?
- Yes, you are all correct. When something is impossible we need to say that we can't do it, because we aren't able to do it. So "I can't" is connected to being able to do something. Every time I think or say, "I can't clean off my desk," I need to respond, "Wait a minute. I am able to clean my desk; I just choose not to do it," which really means, "I won't." Does everyone agree?

> **Wait for response and accept challenges to this concept. Steer the discussion to provide examples that show the difference between being able or unable to do something. Help students identify that we all have personal choices about how we act in various situations.**

- Now we have sorted out the difference between "I can't" and "I won't," we are going to throw "I can't" out of this classroom. "I can't" doesn't belong in an optimistic classroom. We are going to bury "I can't," then have a party to celebrate the birthday of "I can." If we are going to have a grand ceremony to get rid of the silly phrase "I can't," we need to prepare carefully because it's important.
- What do we need for a funeral?
- Let's work together and brainstorm some negative words that the phrase "I can't" makes us think of. Then we can write a litany to help us get rid of the dreaded "I can't." Who knows what the word *litany* means?
- It's a hard word that we don't hear very often. Can someone get the dictionary so we can look it up?

Allow appropriate time. One response may be, "A ceremony in a church where one person speaks and the group responds."

- What we want to do is write something special that will help us bury "I can't." In a litany, the words that the group says are often the same every time. Let's try to brainstorm some negative words to get rid of "I can't."

As students give you words, web them on the board (see figure 11). Have a group of students work together to produce a web using the words they have generated to produce a litany.

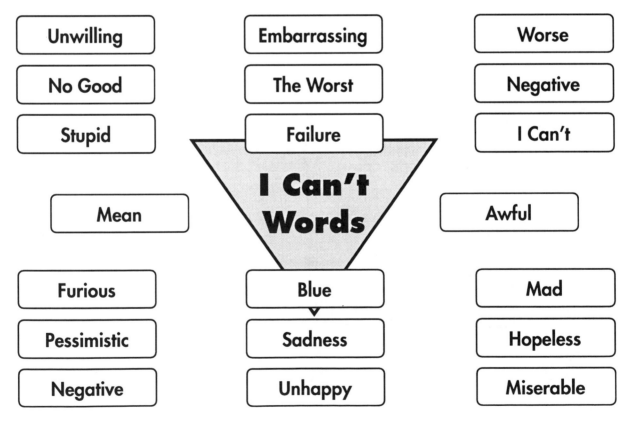

Figure 11. "I can't" web

Name: _____ Date: _____

Let's Get Rid of "I Can't"

Make a list of your personal "I can'ts." When you have finished, cut each "I can't" into a strip.
Fold your strips and place them carefully in the casket.

_____

_____

_____

_____

_____

_____

_____

_____

_____

Be sure you have them all before you put them in

THE GROUND

••• **Activity 5** •••

Hello "I Can"

Student Objectives

- To further develop the concept that we are rarely completely unable to do something
- To reinforce the difference between "I can't" and "I won't"

Materials

blackboard and whiteboard
poster board
colored pens
scissors
ribbon
other art supplies

Teaching the Activity

Explain to students that now they have had a formal ceremony to bury "I can't," they may throw a party to welcome "I can." Divide them into pairs or small groups and ask each group to brainstorm the things that make birthday parties fun. Using poster board, have them create birthday cards and party invitations (see figure 12).

Figure 12. Example of "I Can" birthday card

Give students the following homework assignment. Explain to students that in China, eggs symbolize birth. Tell them to use a hard-boiled egg to represent "I can." Their assignment is to decorate the egg in any way they choose to represent birth. They can decorate it as a baby or as a personal decoration of celebration. Set a date for the birthday party and make that date the due date for the eggs.

Follow the same procedure you used to prepare the "I can't" litany to write a birthday greeting for "I can." At the beginning of the party, have a formal ceremony to welcome "I can." Close with "The Optimist's Anthem" ("I Am a Cockeyed Optimist" from *South Pacific*).

116

••• **Activity 6** •••

Mandala Journals

Student Objectives

- To further encourage self-awareness and explore how feelings affect actions
- To practice using graphics as an alternative to words when expressing ideas and feelings

Materials

guided questioning 10, What Is a Mandala?
one tablet of 11-by-14-inch medium drawing paper
a set of colored pencils or pens

Teaching the Activity

Introduce the concept using guided questioning 10, What Is a Mandala? Stress that there is no right or wrong way to make a mandala. Make your own personal mandala as your students do so. If at all possible, include another adult, such as a parent or other volunteer, in this activity, which will allow you to model how designs may vary from intricately detailed to free abstraction.

This activity is best done at large tables or on the floor. Tell students they may choose any topic they like for their mandala, but the design should be their own. Ask them not to copy what other people are doing because the mandalas are supposed to reflect individual personality differences. Stress that this activity is yet another way of showing how people are different and flexible, and that we adapt to various moods and situations.

When students have completed their mandalas, model how to analyze the different aspects of design. Stress that this exercise should be fun, and that there is no right or wrong way to make a mandala. Tell them to ask themselves, "What was going on in my head as I did this mandala?" Tell students that because mandalas are circles, there is no specific way to look at them. Have them turn their mandalas around until they find an orientation that pleases them. At this point, if they wish, they may label the top of the mandala in some way.

Finally, have students date their mandalas. Tell them that this is yet another way of keeping a journal. For this reason the date is very important. Encourage students to develop their mandala journals by using free time in the classroom to develop new mandalas. If possible, allow certain times, perhaps during art class, for students to develop their mandala journals.

If you have a color copier, you may copy completed mandalas and post them to make a dramatic and interesting art exhibit. This exhibit will be especially impressive for a parent night.

Guided Questioning 10, What Is a Mandala?

- I have a challenge for you all. I am going to show you some designs and I want you to stop me when you can tell me what these designs have in common, what's the same about them.

- Fast thinking. Now tell me what is different about them.
- Good. They're all circles but the designs themselves are different from one another. Here's something else that's interesting. Some circular designs were found in caves that were used by early humans. That makes the designs thousands of years old. Some were used in windows of famous cathedrals in Europe, so we know that they are less than a thousand years old, but they are still very old. Many tribes of American Indians used circular designs, as well.
- What do these designs that are all circles but were made in different centuries and in different countries tell us?
- Excellent. You are all in good form today. It certainly does tell us that people have always been fascinated with circles. At all different times in history and in different places. I think that's very interesting. I don't know why that's so, but it certainly is. Aztecs used circles to make calendars. They chose to record time in a circle.

If appropriate, let the discussion flow freely to allow students to explore the idea of time being repetitive and endless. Students will sometimes become fascinated with recurring cycles. If time and interest allow, encourage students to explore the theme of cycles and circles. Ask them to name as many things as they can that are circular or cyclical.

- I have a new word to describe circular designs and drawings. The word is *mandala*. It's a word we use to describe something that seems to be whole. Usually, if something feels whole to us, then it feels satisfying. If it seems to be somehow unfinished, then it's not whole and it doesn't feel very satisfying.
- We are going to draw some mandalas. From what you have seen, do you think that there is a very definite and correct way to make a mandala?
- Right, I agree. There are so many different ways of making mandalas that there is no right or wrong way. It's one of those things that works differently for different people at different times, in different situations, and in different places. How does this remind you of using our intelligences?
- Yes, it's flexible and changeable. Just the same as we use our different intelligences according to different situations. Let's do a very short visualization exercise involving mandalas.

Music such as *Mozart Naturally*, *Northsound*, *Harmonizing Music with Nature* provides a good background for this exercise. Turn off the lights and have students sit or lie comfortably while you read.

Imagine that you are walking in the country. The weather is perfect. It's not too hot or too cold, but just right. You are walking slowly through a field of tall grass. You can smell the wild flowers as you walk, and the grass is soft as it swishes against your legs. The sky is a soft, pale pink color.

Suddenly you see a huge round shape on the horizon. As you approach, the circle becomes bigger and bigger. Suddenly, without even noticing what happened, you realize you have stepped inside the circle. The soft pink warmth is all around you. You are aware of the whole universe inside the circle. Everything that lives is part of the pink circle. People, animals, fish, and plants, are all melting into the pink circle. Gradually, you feel yourself drawn deeper into the circle. You feel a slight twinge of fear. This is new and unknown to you. As soon as you recognize the fear, it goes as you seem to melt into the pink haze. You are floating with every other living thing inside the circle. Everything feels equal. You are not better or worse than the rose that you suddenly discover you are holding. The pink merges and changes into other colors. Your favorite colors and your favorite smells seem to be everywhere. You are floating around and around in the circle, gently twisting and turning your body as if you were a dolphin in the ocean. Suddenly, you are dolphin, and the warmth that surrounds you is the ocean. You have a feeling of endless movement. Your body is light and flexible.

You pass through to the outside of the circle; you are outside the circle looking in. You see the whole universe moving in the circle, beckoning to you to enter and make the circle whole. You choose to reenter, and gradually you become aware that you are again in the field, but the field is within the circle. You are back where your adventure started, but you understand something new: you, the field, and the universe are part of the circle. The circle is life. The circle is everything that is important to you. You open your eyes slowly and continue with your place in the circle.

Immediately following this exercise, have students draw a circle (see figure 13) and color each section of the circle, blending the colors they saw while they were visualizing. If they claim to have visualized in black and white, ask them to use their favorite colors. They may fill each section with patterns if they choose.

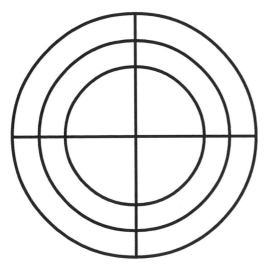

If they choose, they may make their mandalas their personal interpretations of the visualization. For example, they may draw the dolphins, flowers, grass, and stick figures to represent aspects of the story. They can use colors to reflect mood. Alternatively, students can make the designs abstract, relying totally upon the colors to tell the story.

Figure 13. Mandala example

UNIT 5

Discovering a Passion

Rationale

We believe that technology is an important part of each individual's strategy tool box, and that all students must know how to use modern technology with thought and care. It must be difficult, and perhaps impossible, for today's young people to imagine a time without television, video, and computers. The entertainment and communication these machines afford us have become an integral part of our lives.

The great power of this electronic science is immediate feedback. As we discussed this power, we began to realize that one side effect of this instant gratification is a loss of time to reflect on the information and experiences we are having. Reflection allows us to make connections that build a network of experience to which we relate as human beings. It seemed to us that without reflection, most understanding is superficial and may be short lived.

Edward Hallowell speaks eloquently of his concerns that our fast moving society does not nurture the feeling of connectedness that we all need in order to function as healthy human beings. He encourages us to explore relationships of time, space, and human experience to develop the feeling of being connected into a larger experience. His words seem profound and important to us. We determined that we needed to explore with our students the notion of the connection between reflection and feelings.

As we talked, we became aware of how we were expressing our need to communicate these ideas to our students. We were talking with emotion and passion. With a flash of understanding, we discovered that we wanted our students to experience similar feelings. We wanted them to discover a passion and connect their passion to a need to know more.

How, we wondered, could we create an opportunity for our students to feel passion, and how could we relate this feeling to learning and school?

Student Comment

I have so many passions. I want to try so many things. I can think of ways to use my passions forever.

··· Activity 1 ···

What Is a Passion?

Student Objectives

- To identify passions and how they relate to what we do in life
- To nurture the notion of taking time to explore and pursue dreams

Materials

guided questioning 13, Passions
blackboard or whiteboard

Teaching the Activity

Introduce the concept using guided questioning 13, Passions. Encourage students to share their special interests and those of friends and family. During the discussion, ask students to name certain professions that allow people to use the things students feel passionate about. Lead them to identify the various intelligences that are used to explore and realize various passions.

Have students illustrate various occupations and define which areas they believe the people involved in these occupations would need to feel passionate. Have them develop posters or webs on these topics (see figures 14 and 15). When they have finished their posters and webs, have them share their ideas with the class.

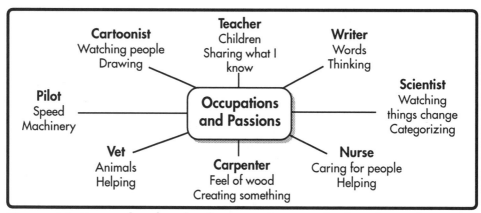

Figure 14. Example of web of occupations and related passions

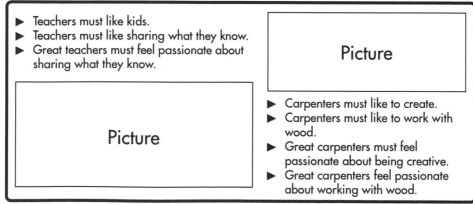

Figure 15. Example of poster of occupations and related passions

Guided Questioning 11, Passions

- Have any of you ever thought about people in history who did some amazing things?
- Name some people who have invented things or have done something that really changed their future.

Create a web as students supply names. In Carol's class, the name *Beethoven* came up.

- What was remarkable about Beethoven?
- Yes, he was a wonderful composer, and we still listen to the music he composed so many years ago. Who knows something else remarkable about him? Something that happened to him as he grew older?
- Here's a clue. One of his senses failed, and it was a sense that we would expect him to use to write music.
- You are absolutely correct. He went deaf. Did he go just a bit deaf or very deaf?
- Right again. Very deaf. How do you think it felt for someone who wrote such beautiful music to go deaf?
- I would agree with you. It must have made him feel very sad. I'm sure Beethoven was very frustrated and unhappy about losing his hearing. Here's another question: When Beethoven went deaf, did he give up writing music?
- No, he wrote some of his most important music after he was deaf.
- Now here's the question. How do you think Beethoven felt about music? I mean really felt in a deep, deep, deep way. How did he feel, not only in his head, but also in his heart? What kept Beethoven writing music, even when he couldn't hear his music?
- Right. Beethoven felt such a passion for music that he couldn't stop writing even when it was impossible for him to hear the music he was composing.
- Ms. King is a music teacher. What do you think is the difference between Beethoven and Ms. King?
- Yes, Ms. King can hear. What intelligence is very strong for Ms. King?
- Yes, Ms. King has very strong musical intelligence. And what about Beethoven?
- Beethoven also had very strong musical intelligence. So what's the difference between them?
- Okay, Beethoven is what we call a *genius*. Ms. King is what we call *talented* musically. Do you think that Ms. King feels passionately about music? Why don't you ask her?

If your discussion evolves in this way, ask the music teacher in your school to share how she or he feels about music. Ask her or him to describe feelings and use vocabulary that evokes a love and passion for music.

- Then do you all think that someone has to be a genius to feel a passion?

- Obviously not. I think you are all right. A passion is to love something that gives you a lot of pleasure. What kind of things do you think people feel passionately about? Do any of you feel passionate about something you enjoy doing?

Develop a web as students give you their ideas.

- Great ideas. How about the various emotions you feel when you are involved with your passion? Let's ask Ms. King how she feels when she is playing the flute. Here's an idea. Everyone close your eyes and pretend to be Ms. King.

Turn out the lights and use the following or a similar visualization.

You are Ms. King. You are a teacher. You love what you do. It makes you want to smile every time you imagine being with your students. They are special people to you. You always wanted to be a teacher. Even when you were very young you would line up your stuffed animals and pretend to teach them a lesson. As you got older, you loved to play school with your friends and you were always the teacher. As you discovered your musical intelligence, you imagined that you would be a music teacher.

Your passion for music never changed, and you developed it and your other passion, which is just important—your passion for teaching. You love teaching, especially young people who learn in different ways. Now, here you are at the end of a hard day. Your optimistic thinking makes you smile and know that not every day will be this hard.

The day is cold, and as you turn the key in the lock of the door to your house, you shiver. Once inside, you glance at the clock and think about the lesson you need to prepare for tomorrow. It's quiet in the house. No one else is home yet. As you pull off first one sleeve of your coat and then the other, you notice your flute case lying on the floor. A wonderful feeling floods through your body. It starts first in your chest, then spreads down your arms to your hands. It's a feeling of warmth and pleasure. You pick up the case. You open the case. You touch the flute. The metal is wonderfully smooth, hard, and cool. It feels so familiar and at once you can imagine the pleasure of putting the cool metal to your lips and creating the sweet sound of a well-known piece of music. You stand up and carry the flute to the music stand that is always ready in your room. You lift the flute to your lips and play the music that you love.

The door bangs open loudly. Someone is home. You glance quickly at your watch. It can't be, but it is an hour later than when you last looked at the time. You feel refreshed, energetic, and excited about tomorrow's lesson. You quickly put the flute back into its case and call "Hello" to whoever has arrived home.

Give students a few seconds of silence before putting on the light and continuing.

- How did it feel to pretend to be Ms. King? What do you think happened to Ms. King in this story? Why do you think she felt so much better at the end of the story than she did at the beginning?
- Good answers. What did her passion for music do for her?
- It certainly helped her. Why do you think doing something we love gives us so much pleasure?

••• Activity 2 •••

The Interview, Part 1

Student Objectives

- To create an interview to be used with different guests who will be invited to share their passions (people loved being asked to do this)
- To further define their own passions

Materials

guided questioning 12, Developing Interview Questions
whiteboard or blackboard
camcorder

Teaching the Activity

Brainstorm a list of various people in the school, such as students, teachers, or administration staff, and people in the larger community who are passionate about various things. Define passions that are related to various intelligences (see example that follows).

Linguistic ....A writer, perhaps an English teacher, who has always loved to read

Mathematical..........A math teacher or the school accountant who has had a fascination with numbers since childhood and uses numbers in unusual and novel ways

Logical ....The science teacher or someone else with a love for the logic of discovery through order

Musical....................A music teacher or someone else who may not play an instrument, but who has always loved listening to music

Bodily-Kinesthetic ...A dancer or athlete who remembers always loving to move and using her body

Interpersonal ....A teacher or sponsor of after-school activities who has always loved being with people; a good communicator

Intrapersonal ....A school psychologist or student who shows special insight into self and pursues passions that are intimate and personal

Spatial ....A design or art teacher who has always loved mapping, diagramming, drawing, or painting

Arrange a schedule for these people to come into school to be interviewed. Allow the guests to prepare by providing them with a copy of the interview questions you will create in this lesson.

If possible, have students videotape each interview. Each student may choose to include part of one or several interviews as a section of their individual videotapes to demonstrate their own passions. Use guided questioning 12, Developing Interview Questions, to help students develop strong interview questions.

Guided Questioning 12, Developing Interview Questions

- Over the next little while, we're going to meet people who have passions. We will discover how they first knew about their passions and how they feel about their passions now. Then we are going to discover our own passions and make a video tape to share our various passions with other people. The video tapes can include some of the people we meet and interview. If some of these people share our passions, we can discover how and when they use their various intelligences. We can also find out if they use what they feel passionate about in their jobs.
- Let's list people who have passions or use passions in their work.
- Maybe some of these people would be willing to come and talk to us about their passions. Before we can get all the information we want from such interviews, we need to develop really good questions.

Post three pieces of newsprint in a row and label each piece (see figure 16). Use the following questions to elicit ideas.

What to ask	What else to ask	What to avoid

Figure 16. Newsprint labels

- What is our main purpose for getting people to come?
- What is our role?
- How do we want people who come to visit us to feel?
- How can we create a happy mood?
- What words will make people feel good and glad they are here?

Write down specific words as students say them.

- Sometimes people feel uneasy about talking to strangers. How can we put them at ease?
- Could we share some of our passions first?
- How can we say what it is we want them to share with us?
- How can we start in a way that's gentle?
- How can we get their permission to videotape?
- How can we get them to share how they feel when they are involved in their passion?
- How can we uncover their thoughts and feelings?

- What things might be upsetting to them? How can we avoid these things?
- What message do we want to convey at the end?
- How can we make them feel that we are pleased with their willingness to share and what they have said?
- How can we communicate that we really understood and enjoyed what they said?
- How can we play back to them something they've said that we especially liked?
- How can we thank them for coming?
- What should we do to follow up after their visit?

At this point, you may choose to continue to work as a class or divide students into groups. Have a group work on each of the following tasks:

▶ **generating a list of interview questions**

▶ **creating letters to invite and thank guests**

▶ **making a schedule for visits**

If students are involved in this planning, they will have far more invested in the activity in general.

⬧⬧⬧ **Activity 3** ⬧⬧⬧

The Interview, Part 2

Student Objectives

- To examine how guests present their passions
- To identify the various facts and feelings expressed

Materials

guided questioning 13, Identifying Passions
student activity sheet 25, Passion Words

Teaching the Activity

Give students student activity sheet 25. Discuss with them the various words they can listen for to help them uncover the information they need. If you have been able to videotape the interviews, have students review each tape after the interview. Use guided questioning 13, Identifying Passions, to help them identify the emotions that the people being interviewed are experiencing as they talk about their passions.

Guided Questioning 13, Identifying Passions

- How did the interviewee describe her passion?
- What things about this passion seem to make this person who he is?
- Were you surprised at how much time she spends involved in her passion?
- Does this passion seem to be one that other people are interested in, or is it an individual passion?
- When he said that it was hard to predict what might happen when he is involved in his passion, did you get the feeling that unpredictability was exciting for him?
- Would that be exciting or stressful for you?
- Were you surprised that she had other, smaller passions that seemed related to the big passion?
- Did he seem to be involved in positive, optimistic self-talk?

Passion Vocabulary

As the guests talk about their passions, listen for these words and circle them
or mark them in some other way. Use the extra space to add any words of your own.

alive	ecstatic	light	_____
assured	ecstatic	lively	
blissful	elated	lucky	_____
brainy	enchanted	magical	_____
brave	energetic	magnificent	
brilliant	energetic	marvelous	_____
calm	enthusiastic	overjoyed	_____
capable	exalted	pleased	
cheerful	exuberant	powerful	_____
clever	fantastic	proud	
competent	gentle	satisfied	_____
confident	gentle	splendid	
contented	glad	superb	_____
courageous	great	terrific	
daring	happy	thrilled	_____
delighted	heroic	tremendous	
delighted	heroic	triumphant	_____
determined	important	vivacious	
determined	important	witty	_____
dynamic	joyful	wonderful	
dynamic	jubilant		_____

Square Pegs, ©1997 Zephyr Press, Tucson, Arizona

••• **Activity 4** •••

My Passions

Student Objective

- To identify what is personally important

Materials

student activity sheet 26, My Island
student activity sheet 27, My Desert Island List
guided questioning 14, Desert Island Visualization

Teaching the Activity

Remind students that investigating other people's passions has been a way of exploring the fact that most people have very strong feelings for the things they care about. Tell them that choosing and researching a topic will give them an opportunity to learn more about the things for which they feel strongly. Focus upon the feelings that passions evoke in people. Discuss satisfaction, pride, and pleasure. Help them identify other feelings that are associated with loving to do something.

Tell students that to start their journey of discovery, they will do a visualization exercise. Remind them to focus on the words and make pictures in their heads. Use guided questioning 14, Desert Island Visualization, to guide them through the visualization. You may choose to play a nature tape as background while you read them the visualization. Read in a way that demands attention: slowly, precisely, and quietly.

When you have finished the visualization, give each student a copy of the visualization exercise with student activity sheet 26, My Island. Keep the mood calm and continue to play the tape. Model for them by doing this activity yourself as they work. Have students complete student activity sheet 27, My Desert Island List.

Guided Questioning 14, Desert Island Visualization

- We've interviewed other people to see what they feel passionate about. Do you all know what you feel passionate about?
- We're going to do an exercise to help you find out what you feel passionate about. If you already know some of your passions, this exercise may help you find others that you aren't aware of right now.

   Turn out the light and ask students to get comfortable.

Visualization Exercise: Desert Island

You are going to a deserted island for one year. There are no people on this island. You will be quite alone. You will be allowed to take ten things with you to the island. Listen carefully to discover what the island has and doesn't have. Think about what you will do for a whole year and what you will need to take so that you are able to occupy your time doing things that you enjoy. There is only one rule about what you may take: You may not take any living thing or any means of transportation.

Here is all the information about your island.

It is a small island. You can walk around it in one hour. You can't see any other land from the island. It is completely isolated.

On the island there is a small house. It is built of wood. The sun has weathered the wood to a soft gray color. The house has a roof made of grass and palm leaves. The grass, too, has been weathered naturally to a soft golden color.

The house is divided into two spaces inside. One space is for living and the other space is for sleeping. The walls inside the house are smooth and white. The floors, which are natural wood, are a rich golden brown. There is no other color in the house. There is nothing hanging on the walls. In the living space there are two chairs. One is made of brown wood and the other, which is large, soft, and comfortable looking, is covered in white cloth. A small sofa is pushed against one wall and is also covered in white cloth. There is a very small, round, wooden table with one chair. On one wall there are book-shelves, but there are no books. In one corner of the living area there is a small kitchen in which there is everything you will need to cook. Pots and pans, a small stove with an oven, a sink, and a refrigerator. There is no food anywhere. The sleeping area has a narrow single bed made of natural wood. On the bed is a mattress, a pillow, and a coverlet. These are all white. There is a tiny bathroom with a shower, toilet, and sink. Outside the house there is a small generator that provides all the electricity for the house. Behind the house is a well with an endless supply of delicious, pure water.

The climate on the island is perfect. In the daytime, the sky is clear and very blue. The sun shines, but it is never too hot. At night, the temperature drops a little, but it is never cold. The sky is very clear and you will see stars that you have never seen before. At about 2 A.M. every morning, a cloud rolls in and drops just enough rain to water the plants and trees on the island. Your island is very green and there are many trees, bushes, and flowers. Some of the trees are fruit trees. There are bananas, papayas, and coconuts. Some of the bushes also have fruit. Nothing on the island is poisonous. There are no stinging insects, poisonous snakes, or other reptiles. There are only small harmless animals.

The island is set in a clear blue ocean and is surrounded by a reef that keeps storms away and doesn't allow sharks to get through. The only danger is outside the reef, where the sharks are many. They bask near the surface, waiting to overturn any small boat.

There are no dangerous currents or jagged rocks inside the reef. The sand is fine and white and there are small coves with wide beaches all around the island. Dolphins live inside the reef. They swim and play all day in the gentle surf. They have no fear of people because they have never been hunted or hurt by humans. Within the reef there are also many different kinds of fish. All these fish are safe to eat, but not easy to catch.

This is a perfect island, but it doesn't offer much entertainment for people other than its beauty. There is everything on this island to feed your body for a year. What will you take with you to feed your brain and your mind? Remember that the island has some important features that can help you make choices about the ten things you will you take. This is an intrapersonal experience. You can choose to find out about yourself and develop ideas and understanding that will help you for the rest of your life. Think carefully and pack wisely.

Bon Voyage!!

Name: _____ Date: _____

My Island

Draw a picture of your island.

Name: _____ Date: _____

My Desert Island List

I will be on a desert island for one year. There are no books, art, writing materials, or musical instruments on the island. There are many things to feed my body but nothing to feed my mind. This experience is intrapersonal. I am able to take ten items with me. I am not allowed to take anything living or any transportation. While I am there I shall occupy my time by

_____

_____

_____

_____

_____

_____

_____

_____

_____

_____

The ten things I will take with me to help me do what I want to do are

1. _____

2. _____

3. _____

4. _____

5. _____

6. _____

7. _____

8. _____

9. _____

10. _____

··· **Activity 5** ···

Passion Project

Student Objectives
- To produce a specific product to represent time and energy spent in research
- To practice the steps required to produce a research product
- To experience the pleasure resulting from time invested in studying a subject about which they feel passionate

Materials
guided questioning 15, Why Research?

student activity sheet 28, Passion Project

camcorder and camera or other materials required to produce a research product

Teaching the Activity
Use guided questioning 15, Why Research? to introduce the concept of research. Provide each student with several copies of student activity sheet 28, Passion Project. As they complete each page, bring the group together to share and discuss their answers.

You will cover the following concepts and skills in this activity:

the definition of research

the connection between intelligences, learning strategies, and research skills

the various research products

how to narrow a research topic

how to develop a research plan

how to define goals

how to develop an outline

how to collect information

how to make a presentation

Guided Questioning 15, Why Research?
- We have all discovered a lot about people's passions in the last few weeks. I really enjoyed . . .

> **Name a passion that was presented in one of the interviews that especially appealed to you. Explain why you liked this passion so much. Lead the discussion to allow everyone an opportunity to name which interviews and which passions they liked, and to say why. As the discussion progresses, stress how much time each person spent involved in the passion and how this time expanded knowledge about the passion.**

- So would you say that these people were so involved with their passions that they hardly realized how much time they spent finding out more and more about their passion?

- How did these various people find out more about their passions?
- By being involved in the passion. Yes, I agree. Let's think about . . .

Name one of the people interviewed whose passion was seasonal or couldn't be engaged in all the time, for example, someone who has a passion for dolphins and spends a certain part of each summer involved in a dolphin study project.

- What did this person do during the time she couldn't be involved in her passion? Did she forget all about it?
- No, of course she didn't. What things could she do to feed her passion while she couldn't be doing it?
- Good, she could be discovering more about her passion. Watching videos or reading. She could be researching to discover more and more about the thing she feels passionate about. How do you think that doing this research could feed her passion?
- Good answers. This person could be discovering more and more so that the next time she is involved in her passion she will know more and enjoy it even more. Think about this. In what ways do you think that researching about a passion could become part of the passion?

Accept all comments as long as they are supported by opinion.

- How do we research something?
- Good, find out information. Where may we look for information?
- We can look in encyclopedias. Where else could we look that might be even faster than a book?
- Computers are certainly very useful. Where in a computer would we look?

Accept suggestions according to students' knowledge and experience with computers.

- All good ideas. In school when do we sometimes need to research?
- For a project, right. A book report. Any kind of report. Which do you think is more fun to research, something about which you feel passionate, or something about which you feel . . . well . . . just okay?
- I agree. I would be much more motivated to research a passion. Sometimes we are required to research something that doesn't interest us at all. Is that hard?
- I should say so. Anyone who has ever been in school can empathize with someone who has that problem. What would be some topics that you would find no fun to research?

Accept all ideas.

- If we must research a topic about which we don't feel passionate, what are our choices?

- Right, we can say we won't do it or we can get on with it. What may happen if we say we won't do it?
- We may get a failing grade. That's correct. But that's our choice. Let's say that we're in high school and we need this grade to pass the year and we really want to pass the year. If we're smart, what choice will we likely make?
- Yes, I think most of us would decide to get on with it. So let's empathize with someone in just that position. How does this person feel?
- Not happy, I agree. So this person has decided to do the research paper, let's say it's a research paper, unless you can think of something else. How can this person be resilient and get into an optimistic mood about this situation?

> **Accept all suggestions. Have the group identify each suggestion as positive or negative and optimistic or pessimistic. Ask them to define how the suggestions will contribute to getting the project completed to get the grade.**

- I think you all have some good suggestions. When you have to deal with this situation, you will do it in a way that will serve you well. I'm impressed by the strong resiliency you've shown.
- You are all lucky because if you can find so many ways to research something you don't feel passionate about, think how easy it will be for you to research a passion. All you have to do is decide on your passion.

> **Help students identify their passions by leading a discussion of personal passions. If necessary, model for them by identifying your own passions.**

- We are going to cover some ideas about different ways of putting together research projects. Look at the first page of your student activity sheet 28, the one that says "Getting Started" at the top.

> **Have students work through the pages to define and outline their projects. You may choose to do this as a class, as individuals, or in pairs.**

Name: _____ Date: _____

Getting Started

In any research project, getting organized saves time. Before you start, decide what strategies you will use to get yourself organized. Finish the following sentences.

Research is _____

_____

_____

Intelligences used in doing research are _____

_____

_____

Two specific strategies involving these intelligences that I will use are

1._____

2._____

Order the following steps according to your best working style, with 1 being the first step. Remember that there is no right or wrong order; the order is what works best for you. Add any extra ideas of your own.

_____ Decide on the title.

_____ Make an outline.

_____ Choose books.

_____ Look for pictures.

_____ Choose people to help.

_____ Map out a plan to get the project completed on time.

My extra first steps are _____

_____

_____

_____

Square Pegs, ©1997 Zephyr Press, Tucson, Arizona

Student Activity Sheet 28, Passion Project (continued)

Researching a passion can help my future by _____

_____

_____

As I read to research, I will change what I read into my own words (paraphrase) because

_____

_____

_____

The strategies I will use to paraphrase are _____

_____

_____

The visuals I will use in my project will be _____

_____

_____

Before I present my project to the class I must consider _____

_____

_____

When I make my presentation, the intelligences I will use are_____

_____

I will prepare a list of questions to give the class as an outline to my project. After my presentation I will ask them to answer the questions. This strategy will work because

_____

_____

_____

I will make this project fun by _____

_____

_____

Choosing a Product

A product is something that is produced. In school it usually means something that you make. Your product will be whatever you end up with after you have done all your research. It is what you have that brings all your research together and presents the information.

In school, the teacher usually says what the product will be. Sometimes, students are asked to choose how they will present their research. If you have a choice, it helps to have lots of product ideas to choose from. Following is a list of possible research products. As you read through, think about the various intelligences required to produce each product. You may have many more of your own to add:

Advertisement	Explanation	Line Chart	Recorded Dialogue
Album	Fairy Tale	Lithograph	Relief Map
Animated Cartoon	Film	Lyrics	Relief-Map
Apparatus	Finger Puppets	Machine	Report
Artifact Collection	Flag	Magazine	Rhyme
Audiotape	Flip Chart	Magazine article	Rhythm
Autobiography	Flow Chart	Manual	Riddle
Ballad	Food	Manual	Riddle
Ballet	Furniture	Marionette	Role Play
Banner	Gadget	Mobile	Science Fiction
Block Picture Story	Game	Model	Short Story
Booklet	Graph	Monologue	Sign
Bulletin Board	Graphic	Monument	Skit
Cartoon	Guidebook	Mosaic	Slide Show
Ceramic	Hand Puppets	Movement Game	Slogan
Charade	Handbook	Mural	Song
Chart	Handout	Museum	Speech
Choral Reading	History	Musical Instrument	Story Telling
Clothing	Icon	Myth	Story Problem
Collage	Illustration	News story	Survey
Comedy Act	Imprint	Newscast	Television Commercial
Comic Book	Information Table	Newsletter	Time Line
Computer Program	Information Table	Newspaper	Tool
Conference Presentation	Instrument	Novel	Toy
Costume	Interpretive Dance	Nursery Rhythm	Travel Log
Crossword	Interview Script	Observation	Travel Advertisement
Dance	Invention	Oral Report	Tree Chart
Debate	Jigsaw Puzzle	Painting	Uniform
Demonstration	Jingle	Papier Mâché	Vehicle
Device	Joke	Pattern	Videotape
Dictionary	Journal Entry	Photograph	Vocabulary List
Diorama	Journal Article	Picture Dictionary	Weaving
Display	Kite	Playing Cards	Web
Documentary	Layout	Poster	Window shade
Dramatization	Learning Center	Puppet Show	Wire Sculpture
Drawing	Lecture	Puzzle	Word Search
Editorial Cartoon	Lesson Plan	Questionnaire	Word Game
Equipment	Lesson	Quilt	Yearbook
Essay	Letter to Editor	Radio Commentary	
Experiment	Limerick	Rap	

Square Pegs, ©1997 Zephyr Press, Tucson, Arizona

Choose three different types of products from the product list.
List the intelligences they would draw on and why you like them.

Product: _____

I would enjoy producing this product because _____

_____

_____

_____

The intelligences it would draw on are _____

_____

Product: _____

I would enjoy producing this product because _____

_____

_____

_____

The intelligences it would draw on are _____

_____

Product: _____

I would enjoy producing this product because _____

_____

_____

_____

The intelligences it would draw on are _____

_____

Narrowing the Topic

Let's suppose that your passion is for animals, and you decide to research this passion.

Is the category of animals a big, general topic or a small, specific topic?

_____

You love animals, but you especially love dogs. Is the category of dogs a general topic or a more specific topic?

_____

You love animals, but you especially want to care for sick animals. Is the category of caring for sick animals a general topic or a more specific topic?

_____

You love dogs, but your greatest hope is to be able to breed Labradors. Is the category of breeding Labradors a general topic or a more specific topic?

_____

Which can be researched most efficiently, a big, general topic or a more specific topic?

_____

Why is this true for you?

_____

_____

_____

_____

_____

_____

_____

_____

Square Pegs, ©1997 Zephyr Press, Tucson, Arizona

Developing a Plan

The general topic of my passion is _____

_____

Specific areas of my passion are _____

_____

_____

_____

_____

_____

_____

I will (check one)

_____ research all these areas in different sections of my project

_____ research one of these areas in depth

I will break my research into specific, manageable sections. These are the sections I will research:

1. Introduction (introduces the topic)

2. _____

3. _____

4. _____

5. Conclusion (draws the conclusions about what was learned in the project)

The product I plan to produce is_____

The intelligences I will use are _____

_____

_____

Defining the Goals

You probably know a good deal about your topic considering that it's a passion. Your project should have three goals.

1. To satisfy yourself
   - ◆ Enjoy concentrating on something you love.
   - ◆ Learn new things about your passion.

2. To inform and affect other people
   - ◆ Give information about your passion.
   - ◆ Communicate your feeling about your passion.

3. Expand your research skills
   - ◆ Become expert at knowing what information you need.
   - ◆ Know where to get information you need.

What will help you get the most pleasure from preparing your project?

_____

_____

_____

_____

How can you affect other people with your project?

_____

_____

_____

_____

List two ways that becoming a good researcher can help you as an adult:

1. _____

_____

2. _____

_____

Square Pegs, ©1997 Zephyr Press, Tucson, Arizona

Becoming a Researcher

Questions to think about

- ◆ What do I already know about my passion?

- ◆ What would I like to know?

- ◆ Where can I find out what I need to know?

- ◆ Who will I be telling about my passion?

What I Already Know	**What I Would Like to Know**
_____	_____
_____	_____
_____	_____
_____	_____

Different types of useful resources for my project are

People	**Books**	**Technology**
_____	_____	_____
_____	_____	_____
_____	_____	_____

It is important to consider the people who will be seeing my finished project because

_____

_____

_____

_____

_____

_____

Developing an Outline

The Table of Contents

Examine the table of contents in any text book. How are a table of contents and an outline the same?

_____

_____

_____

_____

Introduction

The introduction is the first thing you present to your audience. A good introduction must grab attention and make people want to listen or look for more.

For the product you have chosen, give an example of how you can grab your audience quickly.

_____

_____

_____

_____

The Conclusion

The conclusion will
- ▶ show what you learned from doing your research
- ▶ can use words, pictures, or anything as long as it says or shows what you have proved in your project

  Square Pegs, ©1997 Zephyr Press, Tucson, Arizona

Collecting the Content

Explain how a sandwich can be used as a metaphor for a project, story, report, or essay.

INTRODUCTION

The Content

Information: _____

_____

_____

Information: _____

_____

_____

Information: _____

_____

_____

Information: _____

_____

_____

Put the filling in your sandwich by listing some of the information as you do the research to complete your project.

Making the Presentation

When you make a presentation to any group of people, it's a good idea to prepare. Ask yourself questions. Refer to this list to check which of the questions are important for your presentation.

✔ What is my purpose?
     To entertain
     To inform
     To persuade

✔ Who is my audience?
     Peers
     Adults
     Mixed

✔ How much time do I have?

✔ Do I have all the parts I need to make my presentation?

✔ Do I need notes as a reminder of the different parts to be covered?

✔ Have I practiced my presentation several times in front of someone else or a mirror?

✔ Have I prepared a strong introduction to grab my audience?

✔ Have I come up with a really great first sentence?

✔ As I show my project, can I use it to remember all the parts?

✔ Do I have visual elements to show?

✔ Do I have something to demonstrate?

Square Pegs, ©1997 Zephyr Press, Tucson, Arizona

Making the Presentation (continued)

✔ How will I use my voice to communicate enthusiasm for my topic?

✔ Have I practiced pronouncing my words clearly?

✔ Have I practiced speaking loudly enough and slowly enough to be easily understood?

✔ Will my body language communicate enthusiasm for my topic?

✔ Will my audience realize that I feel passionately about my topic?

✔ Can I say something that will make my audience feel that learning about my topic is important?

✔ How will I summarize my topic?

✔ Have I chosen comfortable clothing to wear?

✔ Have I visualized doing my presentation successfully?

✔ Am I optimistic?

✔ How can I relax and have a good time?

Important Facts to Remember

▶ I know more about my passion than anyone else.
▶ I have prepared well.

UNIT 6

Developing Self-Advocacy

Rationale

We believe that our responsibility is to send individual students on with what they need to succeed in the next academic year. In addition, if we can equip them with an intellectual resource file of life skills we have, indeed, imparted some powerful tools.

The concept of self-advocacy is speaking for oneself. The ability to self-advocate rests on many of the things this text has addressed.

Our goal had been to develop students who could successfully accomplish the following:

- understand their specific needs
- identify and accept the elements of various situations
- know personal intelligences, strengths, and learning styles
- set realistic goals
- think optimistically and rebound from failure
- speak up for themselves

The final stage of the program became to provide students with an appropriate forum in which to demonstrate their proficiency and confidence. The end-of-year student-parent-teacher conference was ideal.

From past experience, we knew that preparing for and leading such a conference require many additional skills. We also knew that the personal sense of achievement and the spontaneous admiration from parents is a powerful reward that can result in continued motivation and growth.

Student Comment

 Well it's hard doing your own conference. I never used to know what anyone said. I liked doing it. My dad liked it, too.

••• **Activity 1** •••

Why Speak up for Yourself?

Student Objectives

- To understand why speaking up for oneself is important and to engage in the process
- To stress the importance of the need to
    - ▶ be competent and knowledgeable
    - ▶ make useful choices and personal judgments
    - ▶ be reliable and carry through on commitments
    - ▶ negotiate sensible terms through reasonable compromise

Materials

guided questioning 16, Why Self-Advocate?
student activity sheet 29, Use Self-Advocacy Strategies
student activity sheet 30, Self-Advocacy Response Sheet
blackboard or whiteboard

Teaching the Activity

Introduce the concept of self-advocacy using guided questioning 16, Why Self-Advocate? Write on the board the headings that follow and discuss the meaning of each:

competence/knowledge
reliable carry-through
making good choices/judgments
reaching a reasonable compromise

Ask students to volunteer situations in which they have been able to use some of these strategies or have observed other people using them. If you expect students to be reluctant in sharing personal experiences, share your own experiences or use characters from current reading assignments as examples first.

Have students work in groups to complete student activity sheet 29, Use Self-Advocacy Strategies.

When they have finished, bring the class together to share their solutions. As each group shares their solution and explains their self-advocacy strategies, have the remainder of the class use student activity sheet 30, Self-Advocacy Response Sheet, to rate performance. Have the group continue to suggest strategies and discuss the value of using such strategies.

Integrate the term *self-advocacy* into classroom vocabulary. As often as possible, highlight how various characters in real life, history, and literature advocate for themselves. Have students define strategies the characters used in various situations to achieve positive results or why negative consequences resulted from poor self-advocacy.

Reinforce the personal benefits gained from becoming a good self-advocate, especially for young people who are eager to gain a level of independence. Repeat the idea that people generally treat us according to the way we behave. If we present ourselves as reliable, competent people, that is the way we are most likely to be treated.

Guided Questioning 16, Why Self-Advocate?

■ The term *self-advocate* is really just a fancy way of saying "speak up for ourselves." As an adult, I find that there are many times that I need to speak up for myself . . .

> **Provide an example of a recent situation in which you needed to speak up for yourself.**

■ Has anyone in this class ever been in a situation where you had to speak up for yourself?

> **Accept all responses. As the discussion evolves, begin to use the term *self-advocacy* in place of "speaking up for yourself."**

■ So are we agreed that self-advocacy is something we all need to do at some level?

■ Let me ask you something else. Let's suppose that the bookstore has called me to tell me that they have the book I ordered. I thank them and say I will be in to get it. I am busy and I just don't have time to get there. By the time I go to collect the book, it's two weeks later. They can't find the book. They eventually decide that I have been so long coming to get the book, they thought I had forgotten it and they sold it. I have waited a long time for the book to come. I need it for a project I'm doing. What will I do? What choices do I have?

■ All your ideas are true. I have many choices.

> **Write some of the ideas on the board and work through a problem-solving process to reach outcome for each choice. Be certain to include some negative choices.**

■ Which choice do you think is going to serve me best? Remember, I need this book and it hasn't been easy to get.

■ So what have I been doing while I was discussing this situation with the people in the bookstore?

■ I have been advocating for myself. Now let's think about a situation that has occurred or may occur in school where you have needed to or may need to advocate for yourself.

> **Accept all ideas for discussion. Write the heading *self-advocacy techniques* on the board and create two columns. Label one *successful* and the other *unsuccessful*. Have students decide which techniques go into which column.**

■ Great ideas. Let's think for a minute about the adults in your lives. Who are the most important adults in your lives?

> **Write these on the board.**

■ Parents certainly figure up there as being very important. What do our parents do for us when we are very young? What are some of the ways they look after us when we're young?

■ Does this looking after us increase as we get older or lessen?

■ How do our parents decide that they don't need to do a certain thing anymore? For example, parents feed young children with a spoon. When do they stop doing that? Why do they stop doing that?

- Exactly. When they see that the child can do it. Then they stop. What do you think would happen if the child never learned to feed himself? What would most parents continue to do?

- Parents are sort of programmed to look after their children, because they love them. They are also programmed to let their children do things for themselves when the see that the children can. How can young people show parents, teachers, and other adults that they can do things for themselves?

- Exactly. By doing those things for themselves. One way young people can show that they can do things for themselves is speaking for themselves, self-advocating. Here's a problem. Let's suppose, and remember this is just suppose, that you want to go to a party. Your parents have said yes you may go, but your curfew is one hour earlier than the end of the party. You really want to stay to the end. What will you do?

> **Lead students to identify the two choices of negotiating for an extended curfew and taking the extra time without permission and coming home late. Have them identify the possible consequences of each choice. Lead them to understand that negotiating for an extended curfew and then honoring that curfew will likely lead to future trust and privilege. Identify the negotiation as a self-advocacy strategy.**

- Using good self-advocacy strategies lets adults see that their children are responsible and can be trusted. Self-advocacy is an essential skill for independence.

- Something you will be doing here at school very soon is leading your end-of-year student-parent-teacher conference. If your parent or parents come in for the conference and find you in charge and doing some of the important talking, what do you think they will think?

- They will definitely think that you know something about yourself and the way you learn. How do you think they will feel if you are able to describe things to them that they can't understand?

- They will feel very impressed. What things about school and the way you learn do you think you could tell them that they really don't know very much about?

> **Accept suggestions and supply others that may not be easily generated by students. For example, "Who knows more about the classroom schedule, rules, and so on, students or parents?" "Who understands your portfolio?" "Who knows best how you feel in various situations?" "Who can explain favorite subjects?"**

- Why do you think it's a good idea to prepare for a meeting like this?

- It's always a good idea to be prepared for any situation in which we are expected to do something. So just as I prepare, you will prepare, as well. We will be preparing over the next few days.

> **Continue to encourage and deal with questions and concerns.**

Name: _____ Date: _____

Use Self-Advocacy Strategies

Choose one of the following problems and explain how you would
advocate to reach a solution you want.

1. You want a raise in your clothes allowance.
2. You have just earned your driver's license and you want to borrow
   your mother's car.
3. You have been especially busy and want an extension on the due
   date for an important project.
4. You were sick for an important test. This teacher isn't very
   understanding and doesn't often give make-up tests. You want a
   make-up test.
5. You want a curfew extension.

Number _____

_____

_____

_____

_____

_____

_____

_____

_____

_____

_____

_____

_____

Name: _____ Date: _____

Self-Advocacy Response Sheet

Use some of these phrases to help you get the information you need.
Use the lines to say how well you think the group presenting their self-advocacy strategies is doing. Explain why you feel the way you do.

Where did . . . ?

Describe what you mean . . . ?

How will this affect . . . ?

What evidence do you have that . . . ?

How many ways can you suggest . . . ?

What do you think might happen if . . . ?

How else might you say . . . ?

What conclusions did you reach?

Suggest some other ways to . . .

Give some other ideas for . . .

What is the most important . . . ?

In what way might . . . ?

I think the self-advocacy strategies this group used were

_____

_____

_____

_____

I think this because

_____

_____

_____

_____

••• Activity 2 •••

Resiliency Maps

The following activities will take several days to complete.

Student Objectives

- To identify specific behaviors required to become resilient
- To explore approaches to situations and identify resilient and optimistic behavior
- To continue to monitor inner language to promote automatic optimistic thinking
- To identify information to be presented at the end-of-year, student-parent-teacher conference

Materials

guided questioning 17, Resilient Me
student activity sheet 31, Resiliency Maps
student activity sheet 32, How Resilient Am I?
overhead transparencies of student activity sheet 32
blackboard or whiteboard
colored highlighter pens
overhead projector

Teaching the Activity

Explain to students that they will be presenting the information they have about themselves, with examples of their best work, at their student-parent-teacher conferences. Provide honest reinforcement by praising them for how hard they have worked throughout the year to understand the ways they use their various intelligences and to develop personal learning strategies. Accept any anxiety they may feel about the conference, and explain that they will do many things to prepare so that they will feel more confident. Assure them that you are proud of their achievements and will be there to support them.

Explain to students that they will begin to prepare for their conferences by reviewing many of the activities they have been engaged in during the year. Provide each student with a stapled packet of activity sheet 31, Resiliency Maps. Use guided questioning 17, Resilient Me, to introduce the resiliency maps. You may do so by using overhead transparencies or having students use their packets of maps as reference.

The process will take several days. During this time, encourage students to fill in the boxes on their maps and to make additional notes when they feel it is appropriate. As they work, ask students to highlight in color the statements that seem true for them.

When students have all completed their maps, ask them to discuss how self-advocacy and resiliency are connected. Give students a copy of student activity sheet 32, How Resilient Am I? and ask them to rate their level of resiliency.

Guided Questioning 17, Resilient Me

- Question. What happens to a rubber band after we have stretched it and then let it go?
- Right, it springs back to where it was. This happens because it's *resilient*. Here's something to think about. How do you think people can be resilient?

- This concept is difficult to apply to a person. Let's say it's me again. Something has happened that was a bit of a failure and I'm pretty disappointed, but I've decided that I'm going to use my optimistic thinking. How does being optimistic help make me bounce back and be resilient?
- I first decide whether what has happened is permanent or temporary. What if I went to the beauty parlor to get blond hair and I ended up with green hair. How could I be resilient?
- Right. I could say that it's awful but it's only temporary and have the hairdresser do it again so it will be okay. But here's a harder one. Suppose I was climbing a ladder to put my favorite vase on a high shelf. There I am just about to place it where I want it and, crash! It's broken into a thousand pieces. It can't possibly be repaired. Temporary or permanent?
- Right, very permanent. I've lost my favorite vase. Now, I want to apply my optimism to this situation. It's hard, but I want to bounce back. I want to be resilient. What can I do?
- Good ideas. It's sad, but I'm resilient. I can bounce back. I can say, "Better the vase than me!"
- We're going to use some overheads to look at some ideas of how people can be resilient, that is, how they can bounce back after something happens that is just plain bad. These kinds of things happen to all of us at sometime or another. Again, we have a choice. We can just sink into a pessimistic gloom or we can search for something optimistic and be resilient. With my vase, I could say, "Thank goodness it wasn't me that fell and broke my head into a thousand pieces!"
- Okay, first overhead. "I know how I learn." What would a pessimist think about this?
- Good ideas. Let's start up here in the top lefthand corner. "I know that my teachers can help me, and I am willing to ask them for help when I need it." What does that mean?

Accept all ideas that bring the concept of optimistic problem solving into the discussion whenever possible. Proceed through all the sheets in the same manner.

Name: _____   Date: _____

Resiliency Webs

I know that my teachers can help me, and I am willing to ask them for help when I need it.

I know that sometimes my classmates can be helpful.

I know how to get the help I need.

I don't mind making mistakes sometimes because I know it is a way to learn.

I can get the things I need, such as pencil and paper.

I know the difference between really needing help and just thinking I need help.

I understand my learning style.

I understand what I should expect from other people.

I Know How I Learn

I can tell others what I need to be able to learn a certain thing.

I can tell how other people are feeling.

I know the difference between things that are easy for me and things that are difficult.

I like to get involved in things that help me learn new things.

I can think of organized ways to learn something new.

I recognize when I have done something well.

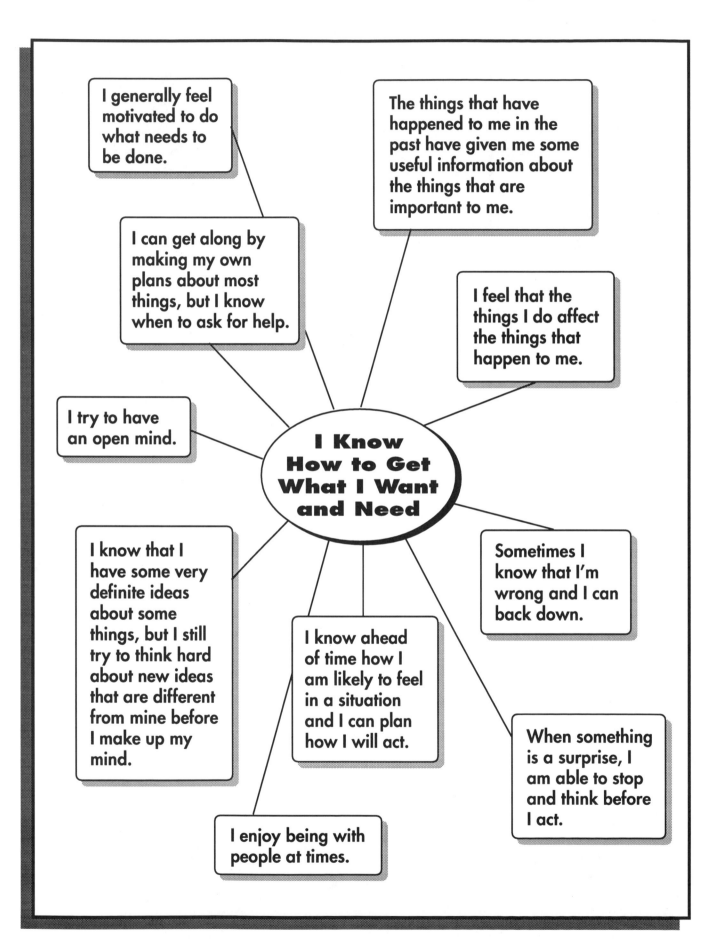

I generally feel motivated to do what needs to be done.

The things that have happened to me in the past have given me some useful information about the things that are important to me.

I can get along by making my own plans about most things, but I know when to ask for help.

I feel that the things I do affect the things that happen to me.

I try to have an open mind.

I Know How to Get What I Want and Need

Sometimes I know that I'm wrong and I can back down.

I know that I have some very definite ideas about some things, but I still try to think hard about new ideas that are different from mine before I make up my mind.

I know ahead of time how I am likely to feel in a situation and I can plan how I will act.

When something is a surprise, I am able to stop and think before I act.

I enjoy being with people at times.

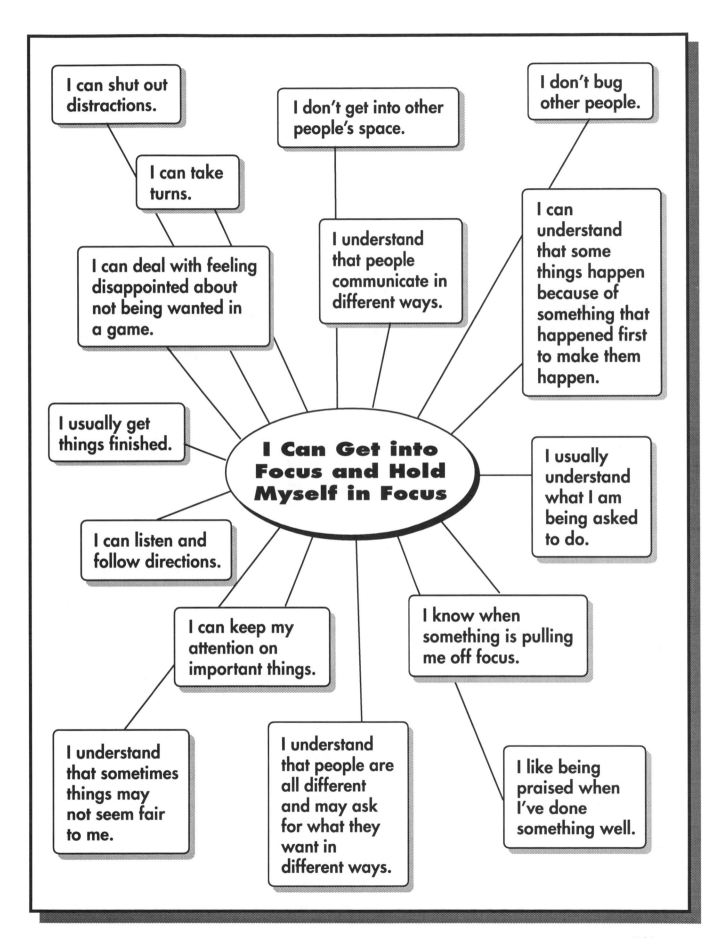

I can shut out distractions.

I can take turns.

I don't get into other people's space.

I don't bug other people.

I can deal with feeling disappointed about not being wanted in a game.

I understand that people communicate in different ways.

I can understand that some things happen because of something that happened first to make them happen.

I usually get things finished.

I Can Get into Focus and Hold Myself in Focus

I usually understand what I am being asked to do.

I can listen and follow directions.

I can keep my attention on important things.

I know when something is pulling me off focus.

I understand that sometimes things may not seem fair to me.

I understand that people are all different and may ask for what they want in different ways.

I like being praised when I've done something well.

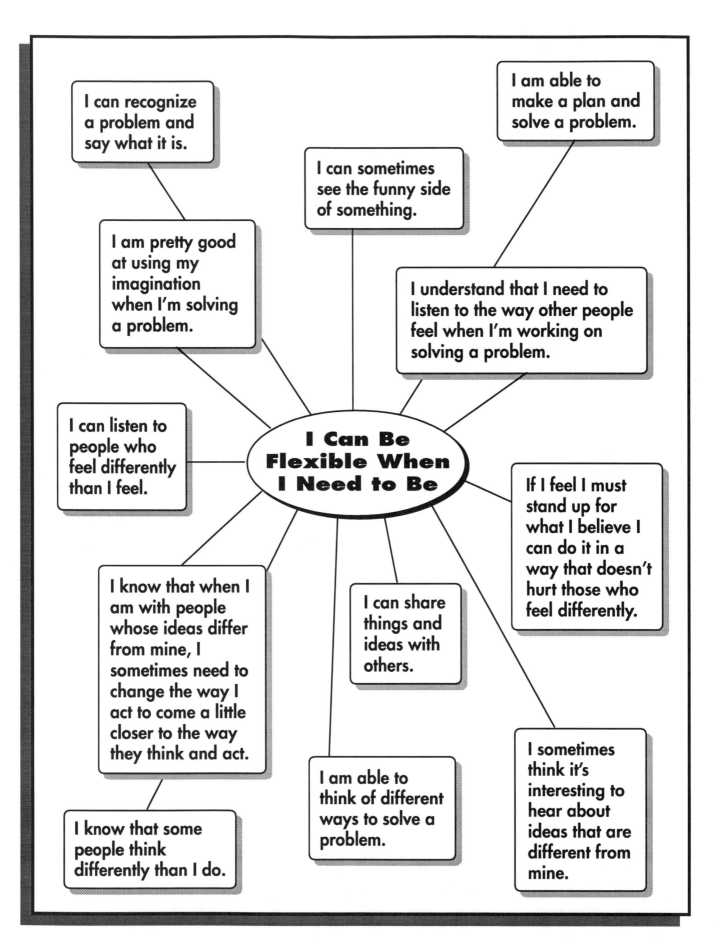

I can recognize a problem and say what it is.

I am able to make a plan and solve a problem.

I can sometimes see the funny side of something.

I am pretty good at using my imagination when I'm solving a problem.

I understand that I need to listen to the way other people feel when I'm working on solving a problem.

I can listen to people who feel differently than I feel.

I Can Be Flexible When I Need to Be

If I feel I must stand up for what I believe I can do it in a way that doesn't hurt those who feel differently.

I know that when I am with people whose ideas differ from mine, I sometimes need to change the way I act to come a little closer to the way they think and act.

I can share things and ideas with others.

I know that some people think differently than I do.

I am able to think of different ways to solve a problem.

I sometimes think it's interesting to hear about ideas that are different from mine.

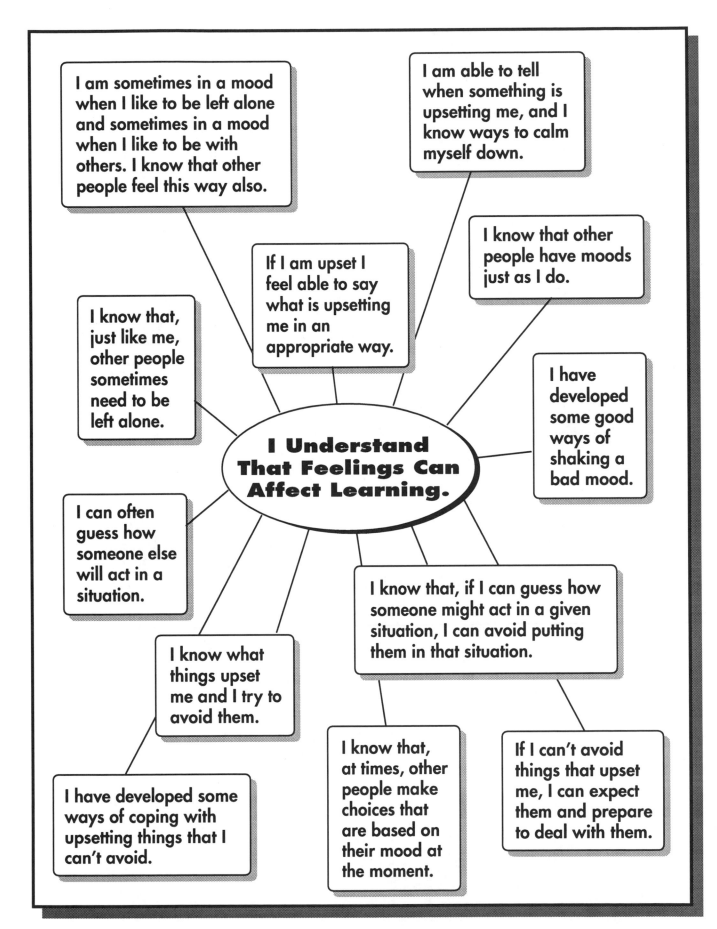

I am sometimes in a mood when I like to be left alone and sometimes in a mood when I like to be with others. I know that other people feel this way also.

I am able to tell when something is upsetting me, and I know ways to calm myself down.

If I am upset I feel able to say what is upsetting me in an appropriate way.

I know that other people have moods just as I do.

I know that, just like me, other people sometimes need to be left alone.

I Understand That Feelings Can Affect Learning.

I have developed some good ways of shaking a bad mood.

I can often guess how someone else will act in a situation.

I know that, if I can guess how someone might act in a given situation, I can avoid putting them in that situation.

I know what things upset me and I try to avoid them.

I know that, at times, other people make choices that are based on their mood at the moment.

If I can't avoid things that upset me, I can expect them and prepare to deal with them.

I have developed some ways of coping with upsetting things that I can't avoid.

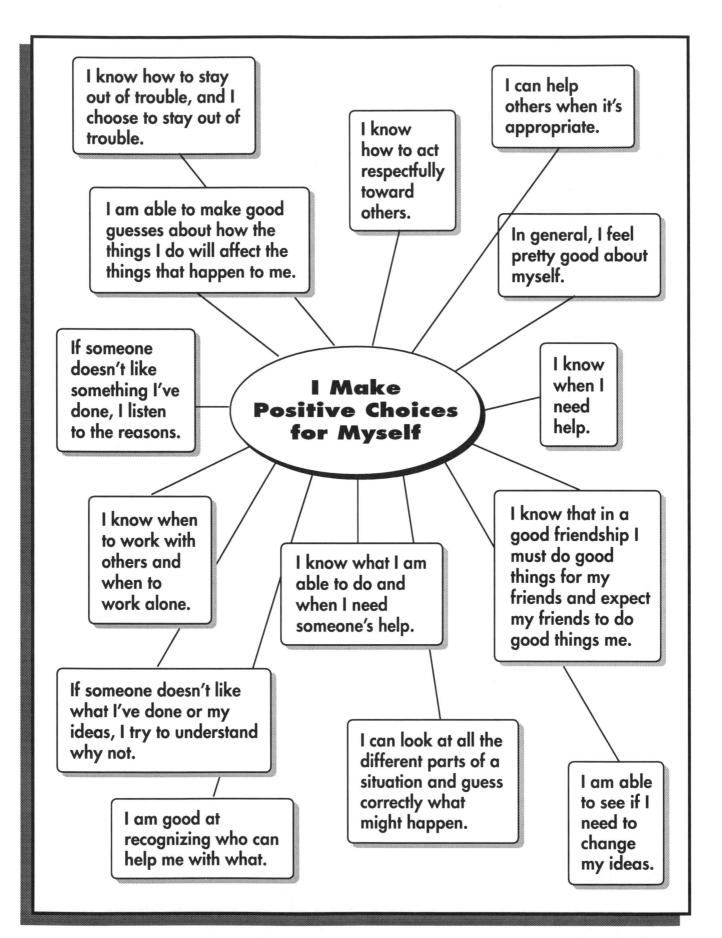

I know how to stay out of trouble, and I choose to stay out of trouble.

I am able to make good guesses about how the things I do will affect the things that happen to me.

I know how to act respectfully toward others.

I can help others when it's appropriate.

In general, I feel pretty good about myself.

If someone doesn't like something I've done, I listen to the reasons.

I Make Positive Choices for Myself

I know when I need help.

I know when to work with others and when to work alone.

I know what I am able to do and when I need someone's help.

I know that in a good friendship I must do good things for my friends and expect my friends to do good things me.

If someone doesn't like what I've done or my ideas, I try to understand why not.

I am good at recognizing who can help me with what.

I can look at all the different parts of a situation and guess correctly what might happen.

I am able to see if I need to change my ideas.

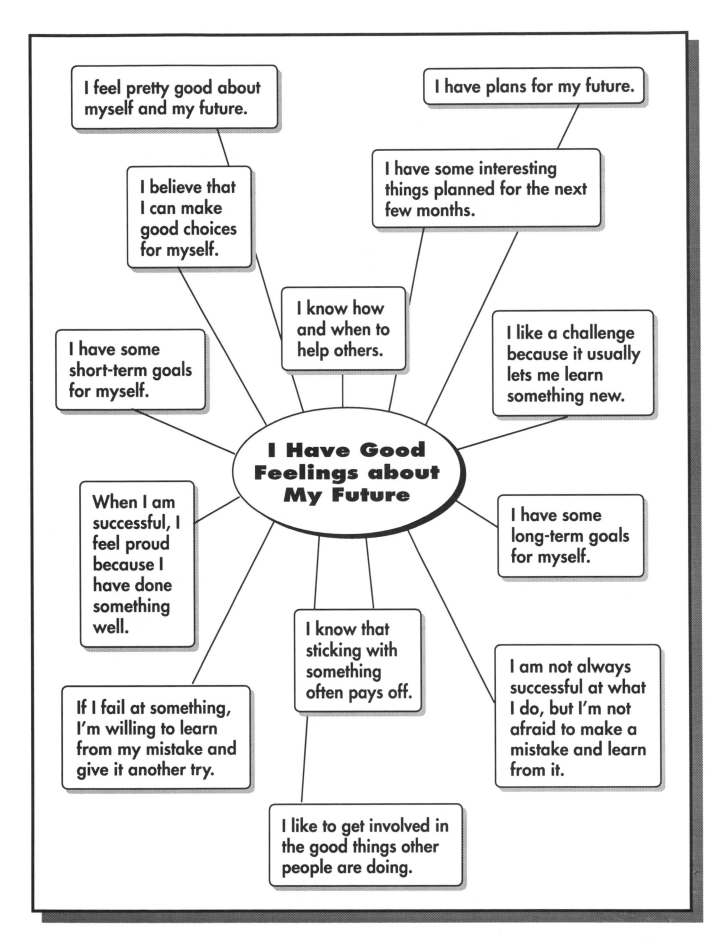

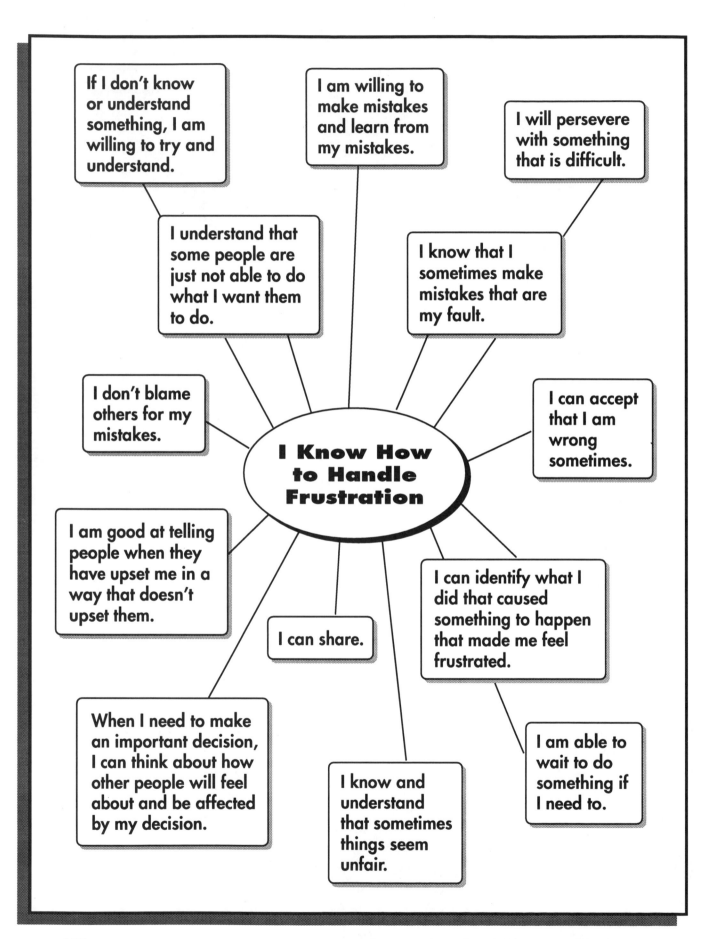

Square Pegs, ©1997 Zephyr Press, Tucson, Arizona

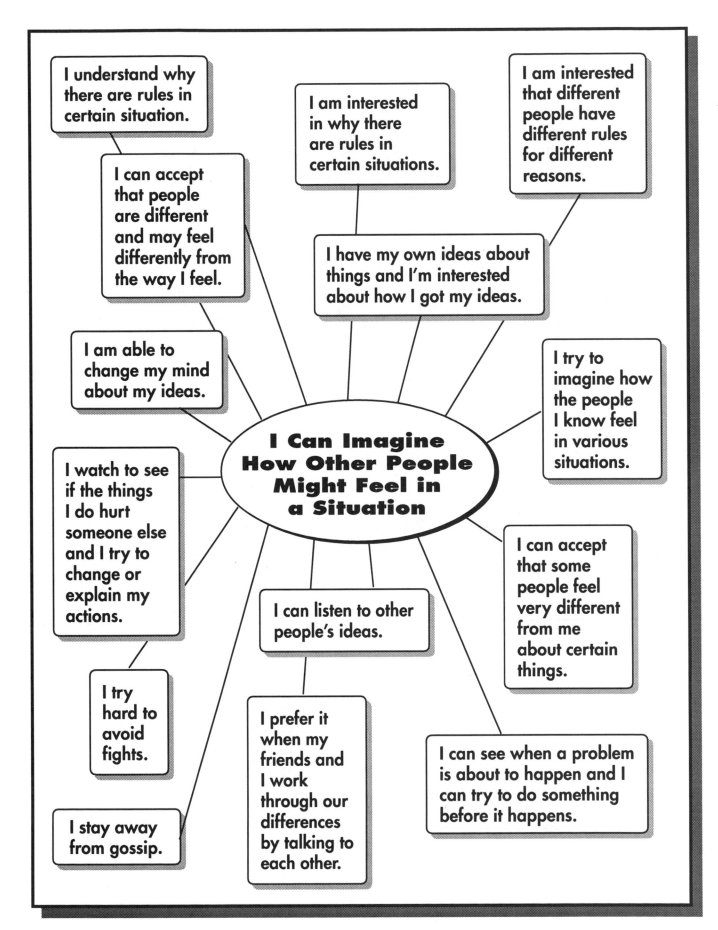

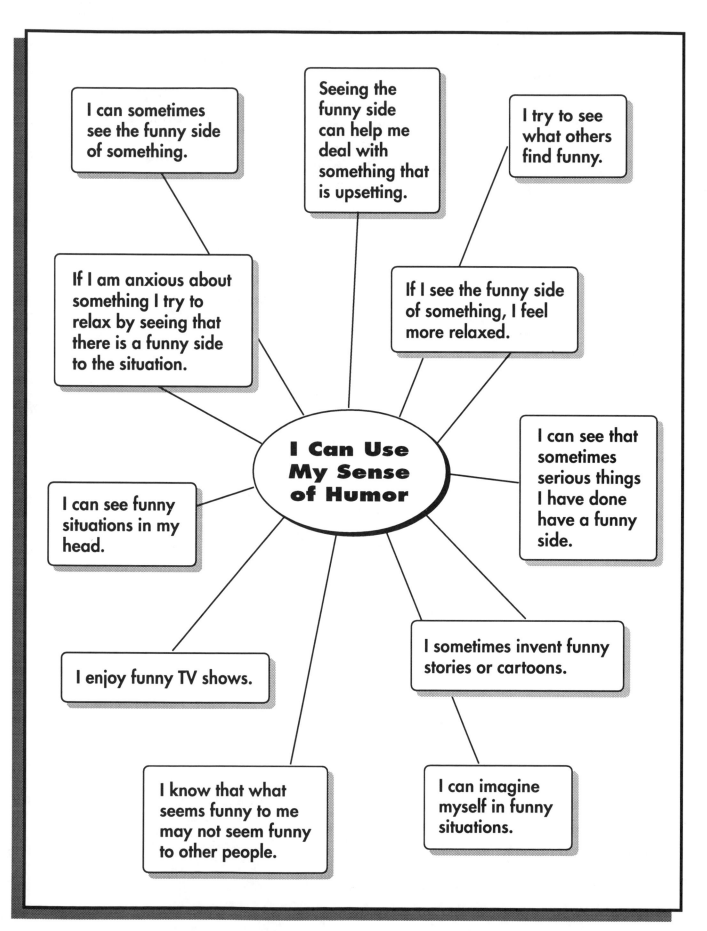

I can sometimes see the funny side of something.

Seeing the funny side can help me deal with something that is upsetting.

I try to see what others find funny.

If I am anxious about something I try to relax by seeing that there is a funny side to the situation.

If I see the funny side of something, I feel more relaxed.

I Can Use My Sense of Humor

I can see that sometimes serious things I have done have a funny side.

I can see funny situations in my head.

I enjoy funny TV shows.

I sometimes invent funny stories or cartoons.

I know that what seems funny to me may not seem funny to other people.

I can imagine myself in funny situations.

Square Pegs, ©1997 Zephyr Press, Tucson, Arizona

Name: _____ Date: _____

How Resilient Am I?

	I know how to learn	I can be flexible.	I understand how feelings can affect learning.	I make positive choices for myself.	I feel good about the future.	I know how to get what I need.	I know how to handle frustration.	I use my sense of humor.	I can imagine how others feel.
Strongest									
Stronger									
Strong									
Beginner									
Prebeginner									

••• **Activity 3** •••

End-of-Year Conference

Student Objectives
- To develop a conference agenda
- To review material for presentation
- To generate and practice language required for the conference
- To organize portfolios in a manner that allows easy access to materials required during the conference
- To role play the conference and define optimistic expectations (this play may be videotaped and reviewed for polishing and improving)

Materials
guided questioning 18, Preparing for the Conference

student activity sheet 36, Me Map

student activity sheet 37, Conference Agenda

overhead projector

blackboard or whiteboard

camcorder and tape (if available)

Teaching the Activity

Make enough copies of student activity sheet 33, Me Map, so that each student can develop a map to answer each Me Map question. Have students write the question in the center of the map and generate a personal strategy for each box.

Introduce the concept using guided questioning 18, Preparing for the Conference. As you work through the guided questioning, make webs, charts, notes, or pictures to reinforce the concepts. Have student complete student activity sheet 34, Conference Agenda. Once students have completed their Me Maps and agendas, have them work in groups to practice the following:

> *introductions*
> *seating*
> *closing*
> *appropriate transition phrases*

If you have video available let each student review her- or himself on video to refine their performances.

Once students feel comfortable with the format and language of the conference, have them organize their portfolios in a manner that will allow them to access the information they will need during the conference. For example, at the front of the portfolio, they may punch sheets and insert in sequence the following items:

> *the agenda (to be removed at the start of the conference and used as a reference throughout)*
> *resiliency webs in the order in which students prefer to present them*
> *the resiliency graph*
> *work samples*
> *other business*

If time allows, have each student meet with you to practice presenting their Me Maps and How Resilient Am I? graphs. Let students know how pleased you are with their competence and confidence.

Me Map Questions

- What are the various ways I learn?
- How do I get into focus and concentrate?
- What positive choices do I make for myself?
- How do I decide which tools and people can help me do something I need to do in school?
- Once I have decided on a goal, how do I get what I need to reach my goal?
- How do I know what other people expect, need, and want from me?
- In what ways am I flexible?
- When I feel angry and frustrated, what strategies help me move past these feelings?
- What strategies do I use to help me understand how another person may feel in a situation?
- How do I use my sense of humor in school?
- What positive feelings do I have about my future?

Guided Questioning 18, Preparing for the Conference

- You all know about some very important meetings that are coming up soon. What are they?
- Yes, conferences. Why are these meetings so important?
- All good reasons. What do we all gain from these conferences?
- Information is one of the most important things. You are correct. Who gets the information?
- Right, parents. How do you think that these conferences help teachers?
- It can help me by making me think very carefully about each student before the meeting. Tell me what your role is in the conference. Why do you need to be involved?
- Good answers. It's all about the student. So how involved do you need to be?
- Yes, very involved is right. How would you feel if your parents and your teachers had the conference and didn't include you?
- Maybe relieved is right! What would you know about what went on at the conference?
- Right again. Only what your parents and teachers told you. Is it ever possible to tell exactly what has been said or how it was said in every tiny detail if you aren't there?
- I agree, not really. How do you get the most accurate information about anything, by hearing it for yourself or having someone else tell you about it?
- Yes, there is nothing quite like hearing it for yourself. Suppose you don't agree with something; can you do anything about it if you aren't there?
- No, you need to be there to say what you think. We know that speaking up for ourselves is important in life. What is it called when we speak up for ourselves?
- Yes, self-advocacy, and self-advocacy is what we've been working on lately. What intelligences and strategies do we need to use when we advocate for ourselves?
- Interpersonal, yes. Why interpersonal?

- We need to communicate with others. What else?
- Why intrapersonal?
- Very good. We can't really get anything we need until we have done a good deal of thinking about what it is we need, and we know that kind of thinking uses our intrapersonal intelligence. I'm thinking about being confident and responsible. What does running your own conference have to do with responsibility?
- It certainly does show that you can plan and organize. Why would you want your parents to see you doing those things?
- I agree. If they see you being responsible they feel good about letting you do things. They are more likely to give you the opportunity to make some choices for yourself. So if you are at your conference and talking for yourself in a responsible way, what kind of strategies are you using?
- Exactly, self-advocating strategies. Talking for yourself.
- Who will explain what an agenda is?
- Right. It is like a list of things to do. An agenda is a very important part of any conference. Why do you think that's so?
- Very good. It tells us where we are going in the meeting. What intelligence do we need to draw on to help write an agenda?
- Logical. Right. Here's an interesting problem for you. Suppose you make an agenda and then at the meeting you discover that everyone else has come with a different agenda. What can you do?
- It's very difficult, but let me ask you. Who's in charge of this meeting?
- Right, you are, because it's your meeting. So who's agenda do we follow?
- Good. That's why the agenda is so important. Let's suppose that this person with the other agenda seems very worried. What can you do to make the person feel better?

Accept and discuss all ideas.

- All good ideas. We could say that we will deal with the concern at the end of the meeting. Very good. So during this meeting do we need to be rigid or flexible?
- It's certainly good to be flexible. In this situation what might happen if we are too flexible?
- Right, we would never get through everything on the agenda. What would happen if we were completely rigid?
- Good, whoever is anxious may get even more anxious. So this is a problem for us. What do we do?
- Great answer. We are not too rigid and not too flexible. We use a mixture of both. You are all going to enjoy being in charge of your conferences I can tell.

Show an overhead of student activity sheet 34, Conference Agenda.

- Let's read through the headings on this agenda. What's the first?
- Introductions. What does that mean?
- Yes, telling everyone who everyone else is and why they are there. At this time of the year teachers and parents have usually met and don't need to be introduced like strangers. What do we do and say? Do we just stand there? Remember, you are in charge.

- Great, that's a great line: "Ms./Mr. A, you know my parents." Let's imagine that there is someone new to your parents at the meeting. What do you do?
- Yes, introduce them. What information is missing if you only give the name?
- Yes, why that person is there. So you need to say how that person is connected with you. You all seem to have done this before. I'm impressed. What's next on the agenda?
- Let's suppose that everyone just sits down before you get a chance to tell them where to sit. What could you do?
- Very good. You could say something like, "Would you mind moving around please?" or, "Would you mind sitting here? I think you will see better." That would tell everyone that this is your meeting and you are in charge. How would you seat people?
- Yes, you want to be close enough to your parents to be able to show them your work samples. You want to see everyone's face. When you have everyone seated where you want them, what message have you given?
- Yes. "I'm in charge." And you are in charge. What's next on the agenda?
- Webs. We've done many different kinds of webs this year. Which ones should you show at this meeting?
- Yes, the Me Maps that you have just done are important. Why do you think they are helpful at this conference?
- They do certainly give a good outline of strengths and strategies. That gives a good outline to help you talk. Let me ask you something else. By now you have introduced or reintroduced people. Everyone knows why they are there and you are beginning to talk about you and how you learn. How will you move from introductions and seating to the next topic?
- Very good. We need words to help us do that. What words could you use?
- Very good. You could say, "And now I am going to talk about webs." We call such phrases *transitional.* These phrases help us move smoothly from one topic to the next.

As you talk, generate a chart or web (see figure 17).

- Let's see if we can list some good transitional phrases.
- How do you want everyone at this conference to feel?
- Good. How else?
- Relaxed. Yes, do you think that they are feeling that way at this point?
- I think that they will feel pretty relaxed and positive by now, because you have demonstrated that you know what you are doing. What comes next on the agenda after you have shown and talked about your Me Maps?
- Right, portfolios. Do you think that we will have time for you to show absolutely every piece of work you've done this year?
- Of course not, that would take far too long. So what will you do?
- Good thinking, pick only the best. Teachers also get a chance to pick what they think is good. You will be able to pick four pieces of work that you are most proud of to show. At what point will you explain your How Resilient Am I? graph?
- Right, I think after the maps would be a good time. What does this graph show?

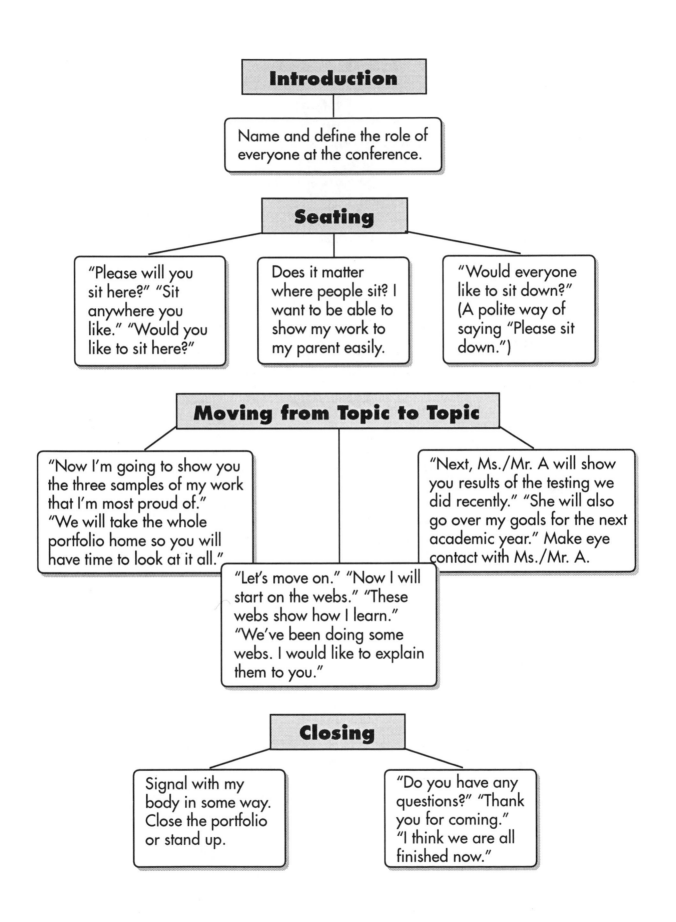

Figure 17. Conference web

- Right, it really gives a good indication about the different areas where you feel resilient. Is this graph like your Smart Profile in the way it changes according to how you feel and the different situations in which you find yourself?

- I think it does, too. Can you work on improving areas on the graph?

- Yes, you certainly can. Why is all this information important to parents?

- Exactly. They just can't understand unless we explain well. How is the graph useful?

- Yes, it's really a summary picture of all your webs. We know that making visual pictures of information is a useful way to explain. What different ways have we used over the year to make pictures?

- Good. Webs, charts, graphs, and drawings. How will you signal that you are ready to move on to your portfolio?

- *Now* is a really good word to signal that you are ready to move on. You can say, "Now we are going to look at my portfolio."

- Good, *next* is another very useful transition word. Give me a sentence that says you have finished talking about Me Maps and want to move on to your Portfolio.

- Very good. "Next, I will show you some of the work I am most proud of." That is a great introduction. Do you think that parents might feel a bit disappointed to be able to see just few examples of your year's work?

- I do, also, so you may want to tell them that, although the conference portfolio will stay at school over the summer, you will bring it home and they will have plenty of time to look at everything carefully. What comes next in the agenda?

- Yes, test data. Teachers do this part. Go back to making pictures. Is there going to be any surprises for you about our testing?

- No, why?

- Exactly, you have already seen the visual picture in the form of a line graph. You can contribute any comments you like at this time, and also for the next thing on the agenda which is . . . ?

- Goals for the future. The teacher gets to talk about this part also, but you can contribute any information you like.

- Very good. That's the amount of time a teacher should take with those items. Why are there no numbers beside the other items?

- Yes, you are presenting so you need to decide upon the amount of time you will need. Do you think the conference should go on for two hours?

- Right, no one wants to sit for two hours over this. How about fifteen minutes?

- Okay, not enough time. There is an ideal time for people to sit and pay attention, and that's the amount of time we want to take, because the last thing we want to do is lose people's attention. What do you think that amount of time is?

- Someone got it. It should ideally be over in 30 minutes. We have to be flexible, but we should really try to keep it close to 30 minutes. Right, what's the next item?

- Closing. How are you going to know when the teacher has finished talking and it's time for you to take over again?

- Good, watch for body language. Make eye contact and watch for me to tell you with my eyes. Maybe have a prearranged signal. So here we are at the end of the conference. Let's imagine that someone has a question. How do you find out?

- Exactly, just ask. Now let's imagine that the questions have been asked and answered and everything has gone very well and everyone is feeling great. How do you bring it all to a close and let everyone know it's over? What is the polite way of ending?

- Good words. "Thank you all for coming. I think we are all finished." How can you let them know with your body?

- Very good. Stand up.

- Congratulations, you have just been in charge of a great conference. How do you think your parents feel?

- I agree. Proud, happy, surprised.

Name: _____ Date: _____

Me Map

Name: _____ Date: _____

Conference Agenda

Topic	Time in minutes	Words I will use	Examples I will show
Introductions			
Seating			
Webs			
Portfolios			
Goals			
Closing			

  Square Pegs, ©1997 Zephyr Press, Tucson, Arizona

Bibliography

Bloom, Benjamin. 1956. *Taxonomy of Education.* New York: Longman.

Bowen, Jean, Trish Long, and Barbara Austin. 1994. *Revving the Engine.* Atlanta, Ga.: L.A.B. Educational Press.

Buzan, Tony. 1993. *The Mind Map Book.* London: BBC Books.

Furth, Hans. 1970. *Piaget for Teachers.* London: Prentice Hall.

Gardner, Howard. 1983. *Frames of Mind: The Theory of Multiple Intelligences.* New York: Basic Books.

Goleman, Daniel. 1995. *Emotional Intelligence.* New York: Bantam Books.

Levine, Mel. 1993. *All Kinds of Minds.* Cambridge: Educators Publishing.

Miller, Lynda. 1990. *The Smart Profile.* Austin, Tex.: Smart Alternatives.

———. 1993. *What We Call Smart.* San Diego, Calif.: Singular Publishing.

Miller, Lynda, and Kerry Ann Ridley. 1994. *The Resiliency Inventory.* Austin, Tex.: Smart Alternatives.

Moorman, Chick. 1992. *Rest in Peace: The I Can't Funeral.*

Perkins, David. 1995. *Outsmarting IQ: The Emerging Science of Learnable Intelligence.*

Seligman, Martin. 1995. *The Optimistic Child.* New York: Houghton Mifflin.

Sternberg, Robert. 1985. *Beyond IQ.* New York: Cambridge University Press.

Create a classroom culture for self-directed and cooperative learning with these unique strategies

ROUNDTABLE LEARNING

Building Understanding through Enhanced MI Strategies
by Ellen Weber, Ph.D.
Grades 6–12

Create a vibrant community of learning where all students learn from one another. Use this unique approach to combine content and collaboration with authentic assessments.

You'll have step-by-step lesson plans and activities based on the latest research into how students learn best. Bring *Roundtable Learning* into your classroom with guidelines for—

- Collaboration among students, teachers, and community
- Exploration through high-level questioning
- Negotiation of assessment criteria
- Roundtable approaches to creative risk taking

1084-W . . . $36

THE MAGIC 7

Tools for Building Your Multiple Intelligences
by Nancy Margulies, M.A.
Grades K–12+

Take your students on a visual adventure as they explore the power of their 7 intelligences. Students work through this colorful interactive comic book to identify which learning strategies work best for them.

1056-W . . . $16 (package of 5)

Quantity Discounts
Sold only in 5 packs

Quantity	Price per 5 Pack
1–9	$16.00
10–19	$13.75
20+	$11.25

ORDER FORM

Qty.	Item #	Title	Unit Price	Total
	1084-W	Roundtable Learning	$36.00	
	1056-W	The Magic 7 (package of 5)	$16.00	
	1056-W	The Magic 7 (10–19)	$13.75	
	1056-W	The Magic 7 (20+)	$11.25	

Name _____

Address _____

City _____

State _____ Zip _____

Phone (_____) _____

E-mail _____

Subtotal	
Sales Tax (AZ residents, 5%)	
S & H (10% of subtotal, min. $3.00)	
Total (U.S. funds only)	

CANADA: add 22% for S & H and G.S.T.

Method of payment (check one):

❑ Check or Money Order ❑ Visa
❑ MasterCard ❑ Purchase Order Attached

Credit Card No. _____

Expires _____

Signature _____

100% SATISFACTION GUARANTEE

Remember, if you are not entirely satisfied just return the item in saleable condition in 90 days and get a full refund of the purchase price!

☎ **ORDER TODAY!**

Please include your phone number in case we have questions about your order.

To order write or call:

Zephyr Press®

P.O. Box 66006-W
Tucson, AZ 85728-6006

1-800-232-2187
FAX 520-323-9402
http://www.zephyrpress.com